Sioux Fall The People

by William J. Reynolds

American & World Geographic Publishing

For Peg, and Meredith, and the hatchling.

MIKE ROEMER

Front cover: *The falls of Sioux Falls.* JEFF GNASS
Back cover: *From rural...* DANIEL R. JENSEN *...to urban.* MIKE ROEMER

Title page: *Night falls over the heart of the city; looking westward across downtown Sioux Falls, "the Queen City of the Northwest."*
MIKE ROEMER

Right: *Hot-air balloons—a common sight during the mild months.*

Facing page, top: *Sioux Falls has 64 city parks covering nearly 1,800 acres—which the residents put to good use.*
Bottom: *Fawick Park, on the edge of downtown.*

Library of Congress Cataloging-in-Publication Data

Reynolds, William J.
    Sioux Falls : the city and the people / by William J. Reynolds.
        p.   cm.
    Includes bibliographical references and index.
    ISBN 1-56037-070-X
    1. Sioux Falls (S.D.)--Geography.   I. Title.
F659.S6R49   1994
917.83'371--dc20   94-28677

Text © 1994 William J. Reynolds
© 1994 Unicorn Publishing, Inc.

Write for our catalog:

American & World Geographic Publishing, P.O. Box 5630, Helena, MT 59604.

Printed in U.S.A. by Fenske Companies, Billings, Montana.

Contents

By the Banks of the Big Sioux River 4

Getting to Today 16

Rebirth 26

The Old Haunts 36

A Sioux Falls Album 64

Leisure 72

      Daytripping 83

      Seasons 87

Book-learnin' 88

Health Care and High Technology 92

Going from Today 100

Where Credit Is Due 108

Index 109

By the Banks of the Big Sioux River

DANIEL R. JENSEN

Above: *No matter the season, the Big Sioux River—"Te-han-kas-an-data," or "thickly wooded river," to the Indians—is a picture of serene beauty.*

Facing page: *Where it all began: The falls of the Big Sioux River.*

Sioux Falls, South Dakota.

The name makes it sound like the sort of town that Clark Kent grew up in. But that was Smallville. Perhaps the town where Jimmy Stewart lived in *It's a Wonderful Life.* But that was Bedford Falls. "Little House on the Prairie?" No; that TV series was set in Walnut Grove, Minnesota.

But at least we're getting closer.

Sioux Falls, South Dakota. Yes, it has that well-scrubbed, middle-American, small-town ring to it. And as recently as twenty or twenty-five years ago, the community fit the connotation: In virtually every way that mattered, Sioux Falls *was* a small town, with all the good and bad that goes with that. Today, however, near the close of the twentieth century and only a few short years into the city's second hundred years, Sioux Falls finds itself at that "awkward age," the municipal equivalent of gawky

Above: In 1992, Money magazine discovered what more than 100,000 people already knew: This "friendly, little-known midwestern city" is the best place in America!

Right: The walking and biking trail through Spellerberg Park.

Facing page: If the pastoral lushness of Sioux Falls' parks and open spaces isn't enough, a short drive will reveal real pastures and inexhaustible greenery.

adolescence. It has experienced a rate of growth in excess of even the most optimistic expectations; it has undergone a sea-change in its economic base; it has become both a regional medical center and a regional financial center; it has, depending on your point of view, enjoyed or endured the distinction of being *Money* magazine's "number-one city"; it has in many ways come into its own. Sioux Falls has joined the ranks of America's "second-tier" cities. And yet it is still, in many ways, at heart a small town. The dichotomy can create no small amount of tension. And no small amount of excitement.

Shall we get some of the dry statistics out of the way first? Sioux Falls is the county seat of Minnehaha County and the principal city of South Dakota. It has a population of about 110,000, according to 1994 totals; 145,000 if you include "greater" Sioux Falls. The median age of its residents is 30.7 years (as compared with 32.2 years for the country as a whole). Its nonwhite population is around two percent, mostly Native American people. The single largest employment sector is the service sector, followed by retail trade, then manufacturing, then government. Because agriculture is a major industry in the state, the Sioux Falls Stockyards routinely ranks among the busiest in the nation. Sioux Falls is the largest retail and wholesale center between Omaha and Minneapolis. It is the 258th-largest market in the country. It is 1,395 feet above sea level and its land area encompasses approximately 38 square miles. It is

184 miles north of Omaha, 237 miles southwest of Minneapolis.

Wasn't that fun?

The "south" in South Dakota, incidentally, serves to distinguish it from North Dakota: it is not located in the South. You laugh, but shortly after my wife and I returned to Sioux Falls (from St. Paul, Minnesota, in case you're interested), we had a call from a friend in the East who was preparing to attend a convention in Arizona and wondered how close he would be to us. This is the sort of thing that can put a strain on a friendship.

For the uninitiated, here's the easiest way to locate Sioux Falls: Get out a map of the United States. See Texas? Count up: Oklahoma, Kansas, Nebraska...bingo! South Dakota, one of those big rectangular ones in the middle of the country. Sioux Falls is near the southeast corner, right where the South Dakota, Minnesota, and Iowa state lines meet, right at the intersection of Interstates 90 and 29. Can't miss it.

(Recently, the local newspaper made a fairly big deal of a national business publication's having referred to Sioux Falls—not the mere fact of the reference, since this is getting to be old hat for us, but the

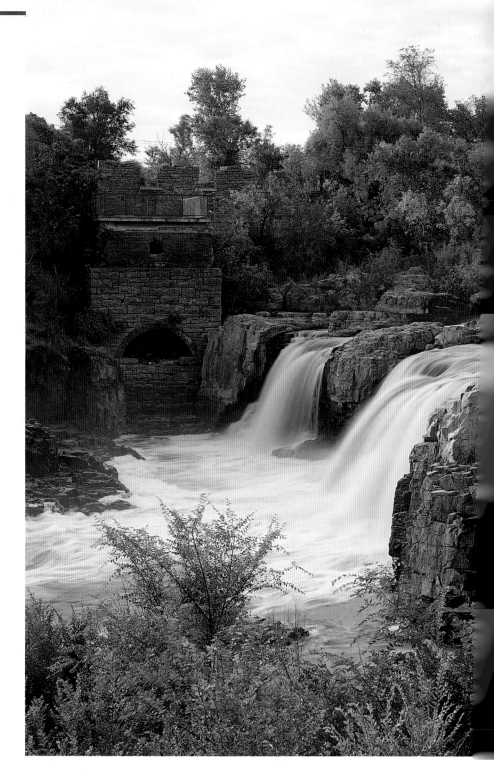

At the top of the Falls, looking east. The stone structure is all that remains of the Queen Bee Mill, for which early entrepreneurs had such high hopes.

8

fact that the reference was only to "Sioux Falls," not "Sioux Falls, South Dakota." This, the paper concluded, was to be taken as the definitive indication that Sioux Falls has "arrived"—Everybody knows where we are! Uplifting a thought that may be, but don't believe it. Every time I pick up the phone to place a mail order, I have to reassure the operator that Sioux Falls is *not* in Iowa.)

Newcomers to Sioux Falls think the land is flat. This is not true. It's *pretty* flat, to be sure, but technically the terrain is the stereotypical "gently rolling" topography of the Great Plains, as fabled in story, song, and sixth-grade geography classes. During the Pleistocene Epoch—which began about 2 million years ago, give or take a day—intervals of climatic cooling caused widespread glaciation across the Northern Hemisphere. When the glaciers retreated from this area, they thoughtfully flattened out the landscape and left behind rich soil deposits that make this one of the most fertile agricultural regions in the country, and by extension the world.

The glaciers also, somewhat paradoxically, left behind huge deposits of stone, an extremely durable pink-gray quartzite

Above: The Queen City gets about 237 sunny days a year—but it must be admitted that not all of them are warm enough for sunbathing!
Top: McKennan Park, in central Sioux Falls, is always an ideal spot for a pick-up basketball game.

Facing page: The Falls of the Big Sioux River are in fact several waterfalls, a series of cataracts over which the waters flow with more force than meets the eye.

DANIEL R. JENSEN

commonly referred to as Sioux Falls Jasper or Sioux Falls Granite. And they chiseled into the stone a river valley where the waters of the Big Sioux River flow yet today. The cascade of the river over cataracts of this quartzite is undoubtedly what first attracted explorers and settlers to the spot. It also, of course, gave the city its name.

By all accounts, the Falls of the Big Sioux River were more breathtaking 150-odd years ago, when the French explorer Joseph Nicollet passed through the region. (Nicollet never saw the Falls—his wanderings took him forty or fifty miles north of here—but others described them to him, and he included in his account of his travels a description of the "beautiful and picturesque Falls.") The Indians called the Big Sioux "Te-han-kas-an-data," meaning thickly wooded river, but today this part of the Big Sioux is by no stretch of the imagination "thickly wooded," or even thinly wooded. As the community was settled, various commercial and civic ventures demanded damming, landfilling, and sundry other "improve-ments" that changed the course of the river and left the Falls today more scenic than spectacular. Nevertheless, the Falls were and are the heart and soul of the city—without them, would there even be a city here today?—and there is no better, no truer place to be-gin to work toward a sense of this community.

To the Falls, then. Season is irrelevant. They are quite beautiful at any time of the year. I have visited there in the middle of droughts, when the Big Sioux was little more than a trickle; I have visited in the

Above: *The glaciers that leveled the Great Plains left huge deposits of pink-gray quartzite known locally as Sioux Falls Granite. Quarrying was a boom industry in early Sioux Falls.*

Facing page: *Sunset on the edge of the city.*

dead of winter, when wind-chill factors were in the neighborhood of sixty degrees below zero and the Falls themselves were a monumental ice sculpture; I have visited in early spring, when the banks of the river seemed hardly capable of holding the runoff of winter snows; I have visited in late autumn, when the waters seemed to join the rest of nature in slowing down and drifting into the long slumber of winter. I have visited there at every time of year over the past twenty-five years or so, and I have never been disappointed.

Still, an unprepared visitor might be, if only because "waterfall" is a deceptive term. It sets you up to expect a precipitous drop, something on the order of the one that Sherlock Holmes and Professor Moriarty went over in their final, fatal confrontation. The Falls of the Big Sioux River are no such thing. Falls—plural—is the right word, for these are a *series* of falls, not so much one big sheer drop as a triple-threat series of scabrous shelves and ledges and outcrops over which the water tumbles, inevitably, toward its destiny.

The Falls themselves are deceptive, too, or perhaps "subtle" is the word. Above the cataracts, the waters of the Big Sioux seem to drift in an unhurried, even lazy fashion. Totally unconcerned the river is, appearing to be going not much of anyplace at all, let alone over a waterfall. Even at the top of the craggy outcrop of Sioux Falls Granite, the water doesn't seem to be moving swiftly. It seems to flow, to glide, over the rocks, rather than to fall. And of course this is not a high waterfall, so there is no obvious spectacle such as the water crashing straight down from a great height, Niagara-like, and throwing back a misty screen. No, the effect is, as I say, subtle. Glance downward, to the bottom, where the green-blue water pauses to collect its wits before resuming its downstream journey. That thick foam down there isn't All-Temperature Cheer; it isn't Barbasol; it isn't Redi-Whip. It's power, the evidence of the kinetic energy in that water racing over those rocks—racing, yes, even if it seemed a moment ago to be meandering. The proof is there: suds don't lie. The Falls have hoodwinked you. In a piece of watery legerdemain that they practice all the time, they have tricked you into thinking they're a pretty, picturesque, but not terribly exciting, bit of scenery, when in fact—subtly, deceptively—they pack a considerable punch.

Over the decades, incidentally, various visionaries and entrepreneurs have observed this same almost preternatural display, and tried to tame the kinetic energy inherent in the Falls. Mills, breweries, hydro-electric plants, factories—there's a long succession of them, some built, some only imagined. None survives today. Each left its mark on the river

The Falls were and are the heart and soul of the city—without them, would there even be a city here today?—and there is no better, no truer place to begin to work toward a sense of this community.

14

There are more than 150 churches and religious/spiritual organizations in Sioux Falls, representing beliefs ranging from traditional to New Age.

and the Falls, but in the end only the Falls endured, and today they exist only to be, as they were in the days of Nicollet, "beautiful and picturesque." Nothing against the entrepreneurial spirit, but this persistence of beauty is to me deeply satisfying and almost poetic.

Almost poetic, too—although I promise you, not *too* poetic!—is the way in which the Falls can be seen as a representation of the city itself, which is to say a representation of the people of Sioux Falls. For Sioux Falls can be a somewhat deceptive locality—or, again, perhaps the word "subtle" is more fitting. To the casual observer, Sioux Falls might seem a sedate, unhur-

ried community. Complacent, even. Not too unlike a score of other "little cities" across the country; probably not too unlike ten score of others across the globe. Like the waters above the Falls of the Big Sioux River, the city itself might seem to take its sweet time getting wherever it may be going; it might seem slow-moving, it may seem even torpid. And this may be accurate enough, if you're comparing Sioux Falls to bigger cities— just as the Falls might seem insubstantial if you're comparing them to, say, Sherlock Holmes's Reichenbach. But, just as the Falls are deceptively active, subtly powerful, so too is the energy in the com-

munity deceptive—not to put too fine a point on it, there's a heckuva lot going on here, and a lot of it you don't see directly: you only notice it after the fact, like the foaming water below the Falls. The surge in population; the emergence of the medical and financial sectors; the *Money* magazine distinction, which for many people really put the city on the map—all of it evidence, albeit evidence after the fact. Outsiders were and are surprised. Insiders are not. We knew all along that the energy was there, latent, throbbing below a pretty though perhaps not-too-exciting surface. Kinetic energy.

Getting to Today

MIKE ROEMER

Looking south from the top of the hill on Minnesota Avenue. The city's rapid growth makes life interesting for motorists and traffic engineers!

HOW THE CITY HAS GROWN.

It is only eleven years since Sioux Falls secured corporate existence; and this brief span of time has seen her grow from a scattering frontier village to a city of 11,000 inhabitants, enjoying all the advantages of a metropolis—railroads, wholesale and retail mercantile establishments, factories, quarries, packing houses, cathedrals, churches, colleges, schools, daily newspapers, street cars, gas, electric light, waterworks, sewers, etc. Twenty-three years ago the first permanent white settler located where now busy thousands are pushing the city toward its manifest destiny. Eighteen years ago, a military reservation embraced all the land on which the city now stands, and which was subsequently pre-empted from the government, but none of it was platted into town-lots until 1871. These statements emphasize the marvelous character of the development which has taken place, and it is only for this purpose that reference to pioneer times is herein made.
—E.W. CALDWELL,
Sioux Falls Illustrated, 1888

History books tend to begin with the explorers, the pioneers, the settlers: The Americas didn't exist until Columbus slammed into them in 1492, right?

As recently as twenty-five years ago—I speak from personal experience now—elementary-school students were taught that the first people to tread upon the land now enclosed within the Sioux Falls city limits were the French explorers and trappers who began tramping around these parts in the 1700s. The Indian people? Oh, well, of course, they were here, too, sort of hanging around in the wings like extras in a school play, waiting for their cues to rush onstage and do something brutal or something noble, depending on circumstances and the point being made.

As recently as twenty years ago, high school students were taught that the first people in this region were the Indians, the Sioux, hunters who followed the thundering herds of buffalo, lived in tipis, and occasionally fought with rival Indian tribes while waiting for those French to show up so that history could begin.

But both versions jump the gun.

The earliest inhabitants of what is now the City of Sioux Falls were a pre-Indian hunting people who lived in and around this area for about 300 years, beginning around A.D. 500. So,

at least, archeologists and anthropologists believe, having studied this people's burial mounds and the ruins of their villages that have been unearthed. Probably they—the ancient people, not the archeologists and anthropologists—were attracted not only by the Falls, but also by the mineral spring that flowed from the hillside to the west, and the high bluffs that made for easily defended village sites. Later, sometime after A.D. 800, an agricultural people migrated into the neighborhood. They may have been the ancestors of the Mandan Indians, and they built villages and burial mounds along the Big Sioux River and elsewhere in and around what is now Sioux Falls. Unfortunately, they left no written record of their time here, and so we know very little about them—including why and how they ceased to live here along the banks of the river.

Still later—in the 18th century—the Indians arrived, the Lakota, driven from the east by their enemies. The Lakota were not the first Indian people in South Dakota, of course. The Mandan Indians are known to have roamed through frequently during the course of their business, and the Arikaras—sometimes billed the first identifiable

South Dakotans—moved into what is now the west-central part of the state before Columbus ever bumped into the Bahamas. But the Lakota, who ultimately drove the Arikaras northward, where they allied themselves with the Mandans, were the dominant force in most of what would later become South Dakota—and most important, for our purposes, Sioux Falls—by the time the white people came calling.

The Lakota were and are one of three major tribal alliances formed of seven major tribes that together form the Sioux. (The word "Sioux" is short for *Nadowessioux*, a French version of a name given these northern plains tribes by the Ojibwa—*Nadoweisiw*—which has been translated as "little snakes." Did I mention that the Ojibwa did not much care for the Sioux?) The Lakota, or Teton Sioux, were the largest of the tribal alliances; they occupied the plains of the Dakotas and Wyoming. The Dakota, or Santee Sioux, lived primarily in Minnesota. The Nakota, or Yankton Sioux, lived on the central plains. *Lakota* and *Nakota* are dialectical variants of *Dakota*, which means "allies" or "friends." This definition may have been lost on some of the early settlers, inasmuch as these Indi-

MIKE ROEMER

*Right: Native Americans,
particularly the Lakota Indians,
remain an important cultural
social, and religious presence in
Sioux Falls.*
*Below: Memorial to the Pioneers,
on the north side of the city.*

*Facing page: Sioux Falls is
situated amidst some of the
richest farmland in the world,
and even given the growth of
"weatherproof" industries,
agriculture has a major impact
on the Sioux Falls economy.*

GARY WITHEY

ans were among the fiercest in resisting the white people's westward expansion.

As to those white people, the reason so many of them seem to have been French is that the Falls of the Big Sioux River happened to repose not quite smack dab in the middle of the French colo-nial region of Louisiana. A French map of the region, dated 1701, indicates that the area around the Falls served as a rendezvous for fur trappers and Indians. Well, after all, it was easy to find and always open.

You remember much of the rest from school, the events if not the dates or the dramas or melodramas behind them: France cedes the region to

18

Spain in 1763, gets it back in 1801, sells it to Thomas Jefferson in 1804. Lewis and Clark float the Missouri River from 1804 to 1806. Nicollet, accompanied by General John C. Fremont, explores much of the territory west of the upper Mississippi River in the late 1830s, and later writes about those "beautiful and picturesque Falls" that he never saw.

There was no permanent white settlement here at the time: by treaty the area belonged to the Lakota and was part of their hunting grounds.

In 1851, the Lakota ceded title to most of their land east of the Big Sioux River. Only then could white people legally establish a townsite here.

And, almost immediately, they did.

Here's the popular story: Along about 1856, a copy of Nicollet's account of his travels lands in the lap of Dr. George M. Staples of Dubuque, Iowa. As if a man possessed, Staples founds the Western Town Company to establish a townsite along the Falls. The Western Town Company engages

Ezra Millard of Sioux City, Iowa (who later would become the twelfth mayor of Omaha), to hike on up here with a couple of pals and stake out 320 acres of land "contiguous to the Falls." And Millard does so.

Historians quibble about that pleasant little story—some say it wasn't Nicollet's pamphlet that set Staples off, but rather Jacob Ferris's "The States and Territories of the Great West," published in 1856; others claim that what Staples really saw was a report written by Captain Joseph Allen, who, while ex-

Quarry in east Sioux Falls, 1888.

ploring the Big Sioux River, camped at the Falls in September 1844. Such things matter to historians, of course, but for our purposes it's sufficient to note that *something* put the bee in Dr. Staples's bonnet, and here came the Western Town Company.

This business of "town companies" is peculiar, viewed from the vantage of nearly a century and a half later. But it was all the rage in 19th century America. Why? Money. The federal government, eager to push Manifest Destiny along on

its way, passed the Preemption Act of 1841, which, among other things, allowed for the acquisition of land for little or no money, provided one made certain improvements and lived on the land for six months. Part of the great American legend is that various hardy individuals took advantage of the opportunity to forge a trail into the western wilderness, stake out a farmstead, build a sod house, work the land, make a life. And, to be sure, plenty of people did exactly that. But it can be ar-

gued that the true beneficiaries of the Preemption Act, and other similarly motivated pieces of legislation, were the speculators, opportunists, and entrepreneurs who saw the chance for easy money. If you could acquire, say, 320 acres for $1 or $1.25 an acre, meet the minimum requirements of the Preemption Act, lay out a townsite, attract settlers to it and sell them residential and commercial lots for anywhere from $50 to $200 apiece—maybe more—well, then you would have turned a pretty fair profit.

That's what motivated the "town companies" that sprang up like sunflowers across the prairie in the mid-1800s; that's what motivated Dr. Staples when he founded the Western Town Company; and that's what motivated the founders of the Dakota Land Company, which sprang to life in St. Paul, Minnesota, at almost exactly the same moment that Dr. Staples was being visited by Inspiration. Like the good doctor in Dubuque, the St. Paul entrepreneurs saw great possibilities for a town at the Falls of the Big Sioux River—not because the Big Sioux was particularly navigable (it wasn't and isn't), but because the Falls offered the tantalizing potential for water power, and if a railroad could be enticed into the community, who needed river traffic? But their dreams were even bigger than that. At the time, most people believed that the Territory of Minnesota would soon become the State of Minnesota (which proved to be true), and that the Falls would be outside its western boundary (which also proved true). The Dakota Land Company investors had it in mind that they could use their political pull with the Buchanan administration to have the as-yet-unnamed—

and as-yet-unclaimed—Sioux Falls made the capital of the new territory that would emerge (the Territory of Dakota), which of course wouldn't do their investment any damage at all.

So imagine how disappointed everyone associated with the St. Paul group must have been when they got to the Falls and found representatives of the Dubuque bunch already in residence.

Ezra Millard and two or three other men had arrived at the Falls in November 1856 and claimed 320 acres of land for the Western Town Company. (One of the party, David M. Mills, claimed another 160 acres for himself.) They built a log house above the Falls and returned to Sioux City for the winter—a sensible plan, given the sorts of winters that are common to this area. The Western Town Company sent another party back to this site in May of 1857, and these fellows were busy making improvements to the claim when the Dakota Land Company group arrived on about June first.

Disappointed but undaunted, they claimed their own 320 acres, south of the Western Town Company's site, and rather grandly dubbed it Sioux Falls City. They left two men to hold the claim—after all, the way things had gone so far, who knew how many *other* town companies were waiting to pounce?—while the rest returned to St. Paul, no doubt working out en route how they would break the bad news to the boys in the front office.

Thus the population of Sioux Falls that summer of 1857 was precisely five: John

This business of "town companies" is peculiar, viewed from the vantage of nearly a century and a half later. But it was all the rage in 19th century America. Why?

Above: *Proof that the local landscape is not flat, but rather the stereotypical "gently rolling" topography of the Great Plains.*

Right: *For nearly 300 years, fur trading has played a role in the local economy; the area around the Falls was historically a rendezvous site for trappers.*

Joseph Nicollet explored some distance north of here; nevertheless, his account of his travels included a description of these "beautiful and picturesque Falls."

McClellan, James Farwell, and Halvor Oleson, representing the Western Town Company; and J.L. Fiske and James McBride, representing the rival Dakota Land Company. Given the mix and the situation, the

cles in developing the town. For one thing, the Sioux Falls area found itself "out in the cold" when Minnesota achieved statehood in May 1858. The land between Minnesota's western border and the Big Sioux

territorial capital. The Yankton settlers had already sent a representative to Washington to lobby against granting territorial status to the region until a treaty was signed with the Indians ceding the land west of the Big Sioux River. And in the end, that's what happened: In 1858, the Yankton Lakota ceded their land west of the Big Sioux River as far as the Missouri River. In 1861 Congress established the Territory of Dakota, and Yankton became its capital.

Barely six years after two townsite companies had unknowingly raced to be first to claim the valley of the Big Sioux River, Sioux Falls seemed to be a dream that had died.

---

potential for conflict may seem great, but Charles A. Smith, writing in *A Comprehensive History of Minnehaha County, South Dakota* (1949), claims that such was not the case: "It may be said to the credit of both of these rival companies, that they were aggressive in developing their respective holdings and the spirit of cooperation was commendable."

By winter of that year, each company had sent more representatives to bolster and support their little contingents. The winter of 1857–58, the settlement's population had swelled to seventeen—more than *triple* the population of only a few months earlier! Talk about a boom town!

Not that there weren't obsta-

River became, organizationally, a "no man's land," outside of any territory, which made it difficult for settlers to figure out how to establish any kind of constitutional government. The way out of this was to petition Congress to form a territory that would include the region, but there was opposition to this, most notably from the community of Yankton, some 80 miles southwest of Sioux Falls, on the Missouri River. Yankton had been established as a trading post on unceded Indian land—the 1851 treaty ceded land *east* of the Big Sioux River, and Yankton was and is well to the west—and the concern was that, because of this, Yankton would be disqualified for consideration for

What about the Dakota Land Company's intent to use its pull with the White House to get Sioux Falls made the capital? Ah, politics. By the time Congress got around to sending President Buchanan the act that established Dakota Territory, Buchanan had his bags packed and was ready to leave office. He signed the papers on the way out the door, but it was up to his successor, Lincoln, to name the capital, and the St. Paul investors had no clout with the new Republican administration.

Still, there were triumphs, to be sure. Congress established a post office here in 1859. The population more than doubled again, to forty by 1860. "Sioux Falls City" was named county seat of the newly formed Minnehaha County at the first session of the territorial legislature in 1862, which meant that the territorial governor, William Jayne, got to appoint a probate judge and a sheriff and a register of deeds and all the other offices that no self-respecting bureaucracy would be caught dead without. But the two-score residents of the little settlement faced disappointments as well. A national economic depression in the late 1850s, which slowed the pace of settlement in new lands and probably kept Sioux Falls' population from growing faster. A long-anticipated railroad line into Sioux Falls from Iowa, which never got off the drawing board. The Civil War, which erupted in 1861. And Indian uprisings.

Remember that treaty in 1858, the one in which the Indians ceded their land west of the Big Sioux River to the U.S. government? Well, one of the many problems the feds had in dealing with the various tribes was that, having not discovered the virtues and advantages of multilayered bureaucracy, the Indian people seldom had a central government or single representative figure with whom the U.S. could deal. So it was that the government made its bargain with the Yankton Lakota tribe, but not all of the sundry groups and bands within the Yankton tribe acknowledged the treaty. And those bands weren't too hot on the idea of all of these white people coming in, "preempting," and selling off what they still viewed as *their* land. It made for some friction.

Enough friction, in fact, that the residents petitioned the territorial governor for, and were granted, a military presence, in the form of a detachment of volunteer cavalry—Company "A" Dakota Cavalry—which was stationed at Sioux Falls in late 1861. But as is often the case, a "presence" was insufficient. In August 1862, the Santee Sioux launched a series of attacks on settlers on the "Minnesota frontier," in the southwestern part of the state. By the end of the month, the violence had touched the young community at the Falls of the Big Sioux River. On August 25, 1862, J.B. Amidon, who was Minnehaha County's probate judge and treasurer, went out with his son to tend their cornfield about two miles north of the Falls. They did not return. Searchers found them dead of gunshot and arrow wounds.

When news of the Minnesota massacres reached him, several days after the Amidon murders, Governor Jayne ordered the cavalry to evacuate Sioux Falls' residents to the comparative safety of the territorial capital, Yankton.

On August 28, 1862, the forty or so pioneers who called Sioux Falls home abandoned the little community. Soon after, the Indians entered and destroyed the town, burning most of the buildings. The prairie grasses began to reclaim the roads and paths that had been carved out. The relentless winds blew, uncaring. Summer passed into autumn, and autumn into winter.

People give birth to dreams, and sometimes the dreams live and sometimes they die. Barely six years after two townsite companies had unknowingly raced to be first to claim the valley of the Big Sioux River, Sioux Falls seemed to be a dream that had died.

Rebirth

DANIEL R. JENSEN

Mature trees—and plenty of them—add to the appeal of the Queen City's older neighborhoods.

Facing page, top: *More evidence that it's a "kids' town"!*
Bottom: *Flower beds in McKennan Park, one of the best-loved of the city parks.*

Since this is not the inside back cover you're looking at, you'd be pretty safe in betting that the story of Sioux Falls does not end on that late-summer day some one-hundred and thirty years ago.

In all likelihood, at least several of the forty or so residents who had been removed to Yankton had it in mind from the beginning to return to their little river-side community at the earliest opportunity and begin the hard task of reclaiming what they had built. Certainly the townsite companies were reluctant to kiss their investments good-bye. And, conceivably, there were other settlers, or would-be settlers, still in the east who had been intrigued by the townsite companies' promotional literature—for, naturally, it wasn't enough to merely claim the land and plat out the town. You had to let people know the town was there, you had to brag it up, and no successful townsite company got that way by being stingy

with the braggadocio—and were waiting to see what happened out on the lone prairie before committing themselves to the big step.

The territorial legislature asked the Secretary of War several times to establish a military post at Sioux Falls, but of course the Civil War was in full swing and, then as now, resources were not infinite. Finally, though, in May 1865, the War Department established a military post and reservation at Sioux Falls, and assigned Com-

In May 1865, the War Department established Fort Dakota and assigned Company "E" of the 6th Iowa Cavalry to take possession.

pany "E" of the 6th Iowa Cavalry to take possession. The installation was dubbed Fort Brookings (at least according to a few sources), but soon after was rechristened Fort Dakota. The reservation was about ten miles from north to south and seven miles from east to west, running roughly from above the Falls westward through what is today the heart of downtown Sioux Falls.

Unlike the previous military "presence," the existence of Fort Dakota seems to have done the trick. Outside of a few probably inevitable skirmishes, the settlers who had returned to what was left of Sioux Falls had few problems with the Indians. For the most part, the Indians who visited were merely en route to or returning from the mineral springs west of the Falls, or the quarries to the east, in southwestern Minnesota, that held the pipestone needed for their religious ceremonies. By the end of the decade, whites and Indians were living in relative peace, if not exactly harmony.

And when that happy state was achieved, the military reservation that had made possible the rebirth of the abandoned community suddenly became an impediment to the community's growth. The military, naturally, had staked out the best strategic location for Fort Dakota; unfortunately, most of it was on the prime real-estate that the townsite companies had claimed ten years earlier. Federal law forbade civilians from settling on a military reservation, or starting a business there, or making any claim upon the land. And so, in one of those little ironies of life, the interests that had labored so long and hard to get the federal government to build Fort Dakota almost immediately set to work to get the government to vacate the darn thing.

Which the government obligingly did, abandoning the fort in 1869 and the reservation in 1870. Something of a land rush occurred then, as settlers clambered over each other to stake out parcels. By now the townsite companies that had originally platted Sioux Falls had been dissolved, but several of their agents and representatives had decided to stay, and now worked to reclaim their holdings. Dr. J.L. Phillips, formerly associated with the Western Town Company and later to be one of the pivotal figures in the town's growth and development, claimed the quarter-section of land that had contained the fort and which today is downtown Sioux Falls. He also bought, at auction, the various buildings and other structures the military had erected. The second Sioux Falls had begun.

You can see, then, that Sioux Falls is a "young" city. For all intents, the current city was born barely 125 years ago, when the U.S. government abandoned the military reservation at Fort Dakota. In the grand scheme of things, on the great clock-face of History, that's barely yesterday. There may be nobody left here who can speak first-hand of the days of the Western Town Company and the Dakota Land Company, but the last of them went not that long ago. And there are surely still those around who can speak *second*-hand of those days. This is a young city—you have to understand that single fact if you're to have any hope at all of understanding the people of Sioux Falls.

Why is that? Because of something that, unfortunately, can be described only as "the pioneer spirit." This spirit is a strong presence here, a real presence here, if only because our "pioneer days" are only just passed. (If indeed they *are* passed. In a way, we are *still* living in "pioneer days," since virtually every week brings a new increase in the seemingly endless influx of "settlers"— who may or may not see themselves as "settlers" or "pioneers" but who nonetheless fit the general description of someone who moves to new or unknown territory with the intention of staying.) This pioneer spirit shapes us, drives us, defines us, sometimes consciously, sometimes not.

And yet "pioneer spirit" defies definition. Or, rather, it has many definitions, many manifestations, some of them quite contradictory.

For instance, ask long-time residents about "pioneer spirit" and you will hear such

> *This pioneer spirit shapes us, drives us, defines us, sometimes consciously, sometimes not. And yet "pioneer spirit" defies definition. Or, rather, it has many definitions, many manifestations, some of them quite contradictory.*

29

Left: South Dakota is one of the nations's top producers of livestock, hay, rye, clover, oats, and wheat.
Below: The Falls of the Big Sioux River are a popular attraction and recreation site—as they were a century ago, and probably for centuries before that!

MIKE ROEMER

words as "independence," "self-reliance," and, interestingly, "conservative." None of them is inaccurate. We collectively, cheerfully, buy into the whole big myth of "rugged individualism," the appealing fantasy of the lone explorer blazing a trail into the wilderness, even though we are well aware of the fact (or would be, if we stopped to consider it) that cooperation, not individualism, was the ticket to successful pioneering. But whether "rugged individualism" existed in history is not the point. We like the idea, we *believe* in the idea, and we adhere to the idea. We are "independent," we are "self-reliant." If we do say so ourselves.

Which tends to make us, as a people, "conservative." Not just politically, though on the whole we are, but also economically and socially and even, sometimes, emotionally. This, I suspect, may be part of the reason there are compara-

tively few truly *old* buildings or other constructs in Sioux Falls. (Another part of the reason, of course, is that Sioux Falls as a community isn't that old. And still another part, to be fair, is that buildings have an annoying habit of catching fire and burning to the ground.) We have this "pioneer attitude" which, among other things, influences us to think that New

Is Better. It's understandable. When they arrived at their destinations, pioneers almost invariably built for themselves temporary houses and other buildings, sometimes little more than shacks—sometimes considerably *less* than shacks—with which they could get by until spring, or until times were better, or until circumstances allowed or

30

Although "town companies" may have been the main beneficiaries of the Preemption Act of 1841, hardy individuals did take advantage of the opportunity to stake out farmsteads in the western wilderness.

dictated, at which point they would tear down the hateful old hovel and put up something New. And even *that* would be considered temporary. On and on it went, on down to today, when my wife and I live in a 90-year-old house that, although hardly an antique, is among the oldest dwellings in the city.

None of this is to say that there's any wisdom in blindly preserving the old for no reason other than that it *is* old—that makes no more sense

minders of our history. (More about all of that later.) But our good conservative "pioneer attitude" dies hard, if at all: We may agree, as we did a few years ago, that we need a new city-bus terminal…but do we really "need" that fancy clock tower on it? (In the end, the clock tower was built. It's very nice.)

This, I fear, gives a false impression of us residents of Sioux Falls. We are not a bunch of flinty-eyed right-wing cheapskates. Some of us are,

gled gewgaws, either. We may prize "self-reliance," and yet if someone in the community loses a home to fire, a fund is established or a snowmobile race or something else is held, or some other spontaneous generation of generosity is undertaken almost before the ashes can cool.

Contradictory? Don't say you weren't warned. For good or ill, there's no short-cut, one-stop, labor-saving way to pigeonhole the people of Sioux Falls. (Incidentally, there's no shorthand way to *say* "the people of Sioux Falls," either. People who live in Chicago may be Chicagoans, people who live in St. Paul may be St. Paulites, people who live in Phoenix may be Phoenicians— and then again, they may not be—but people who live in Sioux Falls are…well, people who live in Sioux Falls.)

So we are contradictory, which perhaps is only another way of saying we are human; and we are changing, which perhaps is only another way of saying we are growing.

Both of them are things that Sioux Falls and her people have always been very good at.

The "second" Sioux Falls is the one that took hold and took off. In the years following the Civil War, the great westward expansion of the country

---

Incidentally, there's no shorthand way to say "the people of Sioux Falls." People who live in Phoenix may be Phoenicians—and then again, they may not be—but people who live in Sioux Falls are…well, people who live in Sioux Falls.

---

than tearing down everything that's old simply because it's old—but just to illustrate how our "pioneer attitude" tempts us to prize the new, often simply because it *is* new.

This has been changing, slowing, in the past decade. The city now has several Historic Districts, and there is a growing understanding of the value of those physical re-

to be sure, but that's not an accurate way to describe the population as a body. That's part of the contradictory nature of "pioneer spirit": We are "rugged individualists," but we are also very friendly and neighborly. We may sometimes feel that the new is superior to the old, but we also pride ourselves on getting by without all kinds of highfalutin new-fan-

32

In the foreground, the original Minnehaha County Courthouse (now the Old Courthouse Museum), commissioned in 1888; in the background, the spires of St. Joseph Cathedral, completed in 1917.

occurred, and the little town by the banks of the Big Sioux River benefited mightily. The years 1866 to 1873 were especially booming. By the end of that short period, the town's population totaled 593. Many of these new settlers were the stereotypically hardy, taciturn, fair-haired Norwegians, Swedes, and Germans whose descendants are still a force to be reckoned with in this part of the world. The town had a newspaper, six general stores, two hotels, two restaurants,

---

Our good conservative "pioneer attitude" dies hard, if at all: We may agree, as we did a few years ago, that we need a new city-bus terminal...but do we really "need" that fancy clock tower on it?

---

two lumber yards, two blacksmith shops, two hardware stores, two meat markets, two wheelwright shops, two bakeries, two agricultural-implement dealers, one paint shop, one grist mill, one livery stable, and one barber shop—leaving us to wonder who cut the barber's hair. Another nationwide economic stumble followed that happy period of growth—and of course there

would be and will be others—but it was merely a pot-hole on the highway of progress. Sioux Falls was on its way.

In 1876, the territorial legislature approved the incorporation of the Village of Sioux Falls, which occupied roughly 1,200 acres. Seven years later, the legislature approved the residents' petition for a city charter, which called for a mayor and council form of government, with two aldermen elected from each of four wards. On April 3, 1883, in the first election under the city charter, Jacob Schaetzel Jr. became the first mayor of the City of Sioux Falls.

In 1889, South Dakota was admitted to the Union. By this time, Sioux Falls was midway through a twenty-year boom during which time the city's population grew at a rate of about 1,000 a year. The 1890 census indicated that 10,177 people called Sioux Falls home.

It's interesting to observe that the city was living up to the promise envisioned by the townsite-company investors thirty years earlier—but in a different way entirely. Remember how they were attracted by the Falls, or, more accurately, by the possibility of harnessing the Falls' energy? It never really came off. An ambitious project—the Queen Bee Mill, which reputedly could process 1,200 barrels of flour a day—opened to much fanfare in 1881. And closed, presumably to much less fanfare, inside of two years. (The burned-out husk of the original seven-story quartzite building remains to this day, and is as much a landmark of Sioux Falls as the Falls themselves.) A second, smaller enterprise, the Cascade Milling Company, opened in 1883 but—except for the fact that its backers also opened the city's first hydroelectric plant, in 1887—it never really took off either. There were other attempts, over the years, to exploit the power of the Falls, but in the end the namesake city built its reputation, and its fortune, as an agricultural and a transportation center.

The railroads came in 1878, when the first train arrived in Sioux Falls on tracks belonging to the Chicago St. Paul Minneapolis and Omaha Railway Company. There would be others—the Rock Island Railway, the Milwaukee Road, the Great Northern Railway, and more—and passenger rail service would continue until the mid-1960s.

This period—the turn of the 20th century—must have been an exciting time for the 10,000 residents of Sioux Falls. But it's tempting to turn it into the usual long list of "firsts"—first hook-and-ladder company, 1880; first college, 1881; first water company, 1884; first streetcars, 1887; first city auditorium, 1898; first hospital, 1901; first free public library, 1903; first swimming pool, 1910; first stockyards, 1917; first airport, 1929—and so on. But to do so is to do an injustice to history, and to the people who built that history with their own hands and hearts, built it on dreams that they first had to force to come true. There are plenty of good books on the history of Sioux Falls and its environs, and I refer you to them for the "gory details" of this community's youth.

As for us, you and I, right now, we've gotten this City of Sioux Falls up and running. We've seen where it came from. Now let's take advantage of our living a hundred years later, and see where the city is today.

J.L. Phillips became one of the prominent figures in the growth and development of the city. When Fort Dakota was vacated, he claimed the quarter-section of land that had contained the fort and today is downtown Sioux Falls. He also bought, at auction, the various buildings and other structures the military had erected.

The Old Haunts

The city has more than its share of scenic walks; here, the path along Covell Lake.

Feel up to a walk?

I would like to show you around the neighborhoods—fully aware that there is a great danger in doing so. Not because these are "bad" neighborhoods. You'll be perfectly safe. *I'm* the one in danger.

Here's the reason: Sioux Falls is, as the cliché goes, "a city of neighborhoods." Each neighborhood has its own tone and flavor, as is usually the case with neighborhoods, and each neighborhood has its proponents or advocates. So if I fail to show you, say, West Sioux or East Sioux Falls or the Irving neighborhood, I risk condemnation. Or worse, even. And remember, I have to live here.

So, with a bow toward prudence, I'll confess at the outset that we won't see everything there is to see; apologize to anyone who may be disgruntled by my neglecting to mention such-and-such neighborhood, or structure, or historic note; and point out, in self-defense, that this is a town rich both in history and in promise for the future, a combination that makes it nigh well impossible to capture in its entirety, like a fly in amber. The best we can do is create snapshots, sneak peeks, and hope that by looking at some of the many parts, we can get an idea of the whole.

We go exploring, then. For our purposes, we'll pretend we have perfect weather, loads of time, and shoes that don't pinch.

The first thing you should know, before we begin our perambulations, is that the Sioux Falls street-numbering system makes no sense whatsoever.

Oh, all right, sure, there's a historical "reason" for the cockamamie system our forebears stuck us with. But as is usually the case with such "reasons," it's none too reasonable. It goes like this: Since the "new" Sioux Falls was built on the remains of Fort Dakota, with the settlers taking over most of the buildings constructed by the cavalry, and since that fort was more or less centered at what is today Phillips Avenue and Ninth Street in downtown Sioux Falls, this intersection came to be regarded as the figurative "center" of town. And so, along about 1886, when the residents thought it might be a nice idea to start numbering buildings, an ordinance was passed that decreed that the numbering scheme would start at Phillips and Ninth, and move out from there in increments of one hundred. "Streets" run east and west, "avenues" run north and south, and "boulevards," "places," "centers," "trails,"

The oldest house in the McKennan Park neighborhood is the Edward Coughran house, built in 1878; it's still a single-family home.

Bird's eye view from the Phillips House, 1890.

"passes," and who knows what all else seem to run any old way they like, and sometimes nowhere at all.

Well, you can see how the numbering scheme throws everything out of whack. If you're acquainted with the street-numbering system of nearly any other North American city, you might expect to find the Central Fire Station, 100 South Minnesota Avenue, at the corner of First Street and Minnesota Avenue. Silly you; 100 South Minnesota Avenue is *Ninth* Street and Minnesota, since the north-south streets begin numbering at Ninth Street. I suppose it's easy enough, once you get the hang of it. But one can't help but wonder whether it mightn't have been simpler, in the long run, to have renamed Ninth Street to First Street way back when, when there were only about two or three dozen streets, tops. Too late now, probably… Anyhow, I suspect this is why we locals tend to use terms like "about" and "right by" and "near the corner of" when we're called upon to give directions.

Assuming you haven't been discouraged by all of that, let's shove on our Reeboks and set out.

The Falls Revisited

Since time and distance mean nothing to us, let's return to the Falls to begin our little odyssey. It's fitting, since this is where it all began.

Curiously, inasmuch as it's both the literal and the figurative fountainhead of the community, the landmark isn't easy to find, at least not nowadays. If the streets cut through, it would be about at the intersection of Fourth Street and Second Avenue. But the streets don't cut through—there's a river in the way. From downtown, the mystic intersection of Phillips and Ninth, you would go north on Phillips to Fifth Street, where Phillips runs out of terra firma; from Fifth to Main Avenue, the next block west; then north again to Second Street, then east again, under the railroad trestle, past the scrap-iron yard, around the bend...well, you get the picture. Tucked away, you might say, although just a few blocks north and east of the center of downtown.

There is a city park here now, mostly on the west bank of the river, with a city park's standard issue of picnic tables and barbecue grills, and a playing field. Three seasons out of the year, the grass in this minuscule Falls Park is a remarkable green, an almost Irish green, soft and inviting and the result, probably, of the fine, constant mist of water that floats almost invisibly from the park's namesake. The main body of the park sits near the crest of the Falls, near the first of their several cascades. The Parks and Recreation Department has thoughtfully provided observation points all along here, nice smooth concrete walkways, iron railings, even the occasional bench upon which one may perch while indulging in serene contemplation.

Of course you, being the adventurous sort, are just as likely to find yourself off the beaten path, picking your way along the uneven and mist-slick surfaces of that strange pinkish Sioux Falls Granite, since there's really nothing to stop you—except maybe vertigo—from wandering right up to the very edge. In fact, there's really nothing to stop you from wandering right *over* the very edge, and it's not so terribly many years ago that I would routinely do exactly that, climbing down the rock-face—it's rough, and the many edges and ledges and shelves make it an easy climb—to be as close as possible to the concussion of water against rock. Kids do it all the time, even today.

Occasionally, new visitors to the Falls—at least, those with any sense of direction—experience the sensation that the river is running backward.

The enterprise failed, but left behind not only the burned-out shell at the Falls but also a sobriquet by which Sioux Falls was known for many years and, to a limited extent, still is: "The Queen City of the Northwest" or simply "The Queen City."

Most Midwestern rivers east of the Missouri run north-to-south, forced along that route by the retreating glaciers. (Where there were no glaciers, west of the Missouri, rivers tend to run west to east. But as you stand at the Falls, the Big Sioux clearly is flowing in a northerly direction. A glance

MIKE ROEMER

During the heyday of local quarrying, Sioux Falls Granite was used for construction and paving in such cities as Chicago, New Orleans, St. Louis, and Detroit. Today the hard, durable stone is perhaps more prized for its recreational than commercial use.

at a map immediately clears up the mystery: the bulk of modern-day Sioux Falls sits at a lazy bend of the Big Sioux River, which flows from the north along the west side of town, loops around the southern portion of the city, flows north through what is now downtown and over the cataracts, then wanders around to the south again east of town, eventually finding its way down to the Missouri River, in Nebraska.

Right across the river is the remains of the Queen Bee Mill, constructed of the same pink quartzite. (As mentioned earlier, the Queen Bee Mill was never a success—some say because area farmers couldn't raise enough wheat to satisfy the mill's capacity, some say because the river was never sufficiently powerful to run the mill at its optimum capacity. Either way, the enterprise failed, but left behind not only the burned-out shell at the Falls but also a sobriquet by which Sioux Falls was known for many years and, to a limited extent, still is: "The Queen City of the Northwest" or simply "The Queen City.") There's another observation post over there, but—even though this bluff is higher than the one on the west side of the river—the view is better from the west side.

Despite the fact that the Falls' energy was never suc-

Above: The home of R.F. Pettigrew, one of the founders of the city, is today the Pettigrew Museum. Like most of the city's earliest buildings, it makes copious use of Sioux Falls Granite. **Top:** *Whittier Middle School, in eastern Sioux Falls, is one of the city's oldest school buildings.*

41

cessfully harnessed, the area around the Falls is nevertheless an industrial neighborhood. There's the scrap-metal operation just west of the park; a little north and west there's another metal and plastic recycling enterprise. Northern States Power, which supplies electricity to the community, has a substation on the east side of the Falls. The Sioux Falls Stockyards (one of the busiest in the nation) and the John Morrell Company packing plant (until very recently the city's largest employer) are each just north of the Falls. The neighborhood is dotted with garages, warehouses, dispatch centers. But in the park, standing on the rocks above the incessant swirl and tumult, it's easy to ignore those things and imagine how the Falls must have been a hundred and forty years ago.

Although it does require some imagination. It was "thickly wooded," remember? Hardly that today. And there was an island, eventually called Seney Island, it too wooded and situated at the head of the cascade. This was a popular recreation spot for early settlers, shaded as it was with large trees; a scenic and peaceful place, from all accounts. But in 1907 a dam was built for a hydroelectric plant—yet another bid to harness the river's power—and the river was diverted away from the island. The land's owner, A.G. Seney, sold it to the Milwaukee Railway Company, which subsequently built a rail yard on it.

There were quarries here, too, in those early days of madcap development and entrepreneurism. Not too much of a surprise, that, when you realize that half the buildings in town—or at least those constructed before the mid part of the 20th century—are constructed all or in part of that so-called Sioux Falls Granite or Sioux Falls Jasper, that extremely durable pinkish quartzite so prevalent around the Falls. In fact, quarrying was a major part of the Sioux Falls economy on into the early days of this century. The Seney Quarry was right here, along the river, at Fifth Street. Elsewhere nearby there were Monarch Quarries, Bennett Quarry, Coats Quarry, McGarraugh Quarry, and others. Some of their successors are in business yet today, but as concrete companies; the heyday of local quarrying passed some eighty years ago. Before that happened, though, our little town was a big player in the game, providing rough-cut and finished stone for construction as well as paving blocks that were used to build streets not only in Sioux Falls but as far away as Omaha, Chicago, New Orleans, Detroit, and St. Louis. You only have to look around to see plenty of evidence of the construction, and there is still a half-block-long stretch of street in this town that is paved with the original Sioux Falls Granite blocks.

Today there are plans hatching for sprucing up Falls Park, giving the whole area a face-lift all the way from downtown to the cataract itself—"Phillips to the Falls" is the catch phrase, Phillips Avenue being downtown's riverfront street. The aim is to turn it into a more inviting recreational center, in general giving it its due as the provenience of the city. No one can fault the proponents' intentions. But a sentimentalist has to wonder whether it will be anything to rival the original.

Downtown

The walk back toward the heart of downtown, on North Main Avenue, is another stroll through a quasi-industrial neighborhood. If we had taken this walk a few years ago, I'd have pointed out the imposing building of Sioux Falls Granite just behind us, at 801

An ambitious project—the Queen Bee Mill, which reputedly could process 1,200 barrels of flour a day—opened to much fanfare in 1881. And closed, presumably to much less fanfare, inside of two years.

North Main: the former Sioux Falls Brewery, one of the first manufacturing enterprises in the young city. It opened in 1879, closed eleven years later when the state voted dry, reopened in 1897 when the amendment was repealed, and operated until national prohibition was enacted in 1919. Subsequently the building housed several other enterprises; however, it had been vacant for several years when it burned down, alas, in the late 1980s.

Fortunately, not all the noteworthy old buildings in town have fallen or been pulled down. A couple of more blocks south on Main, and we find ourselves in one of the Sioux Falls' four historic districts, the appropriately named Old Courthouse and Warehouse Historic District. A surprising number of the warehouses are still in use, as warehouses and manufacturing centers; one or two of them are given over to retail; a couple have been or are in the process of being converted to office space. Most of these are constructed of that indigenous rock, the so-called Sioux Falls Granite that was pried from the earth in such great quantities. As you might expect of warehouses, they are heavy, imposing structures; although seldom more than two or three

43

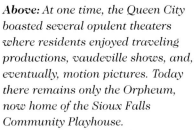

Above: At one time, the Queen City boasted several opulent theaters where residents enjoyed traveling productions, vaudeville shows, and, eventually, motion pictures. Today there remains only the Orpheum, now home of the Sioux Falls Community Playhouse.
Right: A closer look at downtown as a financial center—Western Bank.

stories, they have a definite presence. They seem to have been built by people who intended to stay a good long while, and expected their buildings to do the same.

On Main Avenue at Sixth Street is the original Minnehaha County Courthouse, commissioned in 1888, when voters approved a bond issue to build a courthouse of "Sioux Falls Jasper on a solid rock foundation, with east and south fronts; three stories including basement; cost not to exceed $80,000." A local ar-

chitect, W.L. Dow, designed it—just as he designed darn near everything of any significance at the time—and the Sioux Falls Granite Company built it. Government contracts evidently were every bit as binding a hundred years ago as the are today, since the "$80,000" building ended up costing more than $100,000. But we probably got our money's worth: the county occupied the building from 1890 until 1962, when offices moved to their current location one block west. Now the

224 CITY HALL

COASTERS
SKATEBOARDS
BICYCLES
ROLLER SKATES
PROHIBITED

City Hall—Sioux Falls' first and—so far—only city hall, commissioned in 1934 as a Works Progress Administration (WPA) project. This interesting Art Deco structure is one of only a few pre-World War II public buildings that are not built of Sioux Falls Granite!

45

stately old building with its distinctive clock tower houses the Old Courthouse Museum, which not only hosts the sort of our-town-in-retrospect exhibits that you might expect, but also provides an interesting and unusual location for meetings and receptions in the stately old courtroom itself, which recently has been restored to its 1880s elegance.

As we drift farther south into the bustling heart of downtown, you may notice a couple of things. First, you may notice that Sioux Falls' downtown district is a pretty busy place. Good luck finding a parking space on a pleasant afternoon. This was not always the case. Like a lot of other American cities—perhaps most other cities—Sioux Falls' downtown area was the undisputed commercial center of town until well into the 1960s. In the later years of that decade, though, our fair city joined any number of others that found themselves invaded by that downtown-eating entity known as The Mall. In our case, it was the Western Mall, which opened in 1968 in what was theretofore the no-man's land southwest of the intersection of 41st Street and Western Avenue. (Most of that area had still been farmland until then; only 40 years earlier, the same location had been the site of Sioux Fall's first airport.) Only five years later, an even bigger mall, The Empire, opened its many doors still farther west along 41st Street.

There began a near twenty-year doldrums for downtown Sioux Falls. Many venerable local and national retail establishments moved to The Mall, or folded, or both. Office complexes sprang up on the south and southwest ends of town, to be nearer where the people were. Housing boomed out on that end of town, and the residents found themselves at least psychologically far removed from downtown. If an extraterrestrial spaceship happened to put down at, say, Phillips and Ninth—and there'd have been little trouble finding a parking spot in those days—its occupants could have been forgiven if they concluded they had landed in a town named For Lease, since that's what all the signs proclaimed.

Of course attempts were made to lure shoppers back, but most such attempts were half-baked, or halfhearted, or underfinanced, and none of them worked. Phillips Avenue between Ninth and Eleventh Streets was closed to traffic and turned into a "downtown mall," albeit one that was never completed. Ho-hum. Entrepreneurs tried to turn a couple of the big old downtown department-store buildings into "malls." Right. A hodgepodge of dubious "specialty" stores crammed into the old Penney's building offered little to lure shoppers—and besides, parking was free at the "real" malls. In the middle of the doldrums, in the mid-1970s, I was a student at Washington High School downtown, and take it from me, the landscape was bleak.

Happily, though, the situation is quite otherwise today. And I'm not sure that anyone really knows why. Undoubtedly, it was partly luck: America's great love affair with its malls waned, and downtown Sioux Falls had not sunk so far that it couldn't pull itself back up. And partly it was the fact that over those twenty or so years, the complexion of Sioux Falls had changed: the town had grown, and it had begun to emerge as a regional financial center. And financial institutions, as a rule, like downtowns. True, there's plenty of retailing and restaurateuring going on downtown today, but we also see the imposing edifices of banks, brokerages, insurance companies, and ancillary businesses.

Which brings us around to the second thing that you may notice about downtown Sioux Falls, and that is that the aforementioned "imposing edifices" may be imposing in breadth, but never in height. The tallest building in town, the US West building on Dakota Avenue and Tenth Street, is eleven stories. That's it. Eleven stories. When I was at Creighton University, we had basketball players who were taller. Hereabouts, we just don't go in for skyscrapers. There probably are a lot of reasons, but near the top has got to be the simple fact that we have a fair amount of land, and it's reasonably inexpensive—or, at least, inexpensive enough that when developers compute the extra costs associated with putting up a taller structure, it may make more sense to build three three-story buildings than one nine-story building. Anyhow, whatever the reasons, you won't get whiplash looking up at the tops of any of our downtown.

Speaking of landmarks, there's one right here, at the corner of Ninth and Main—the Security Bank Building. There's no longer a bank here, but when there was—in 1934, to be specific—said bank found itself alleviated of about $46,000 by a bunch of armed bandits who were and are thought to have been part of John Dillinger's gang. It's never been proven that Dillinger

himself was among them, but the holdup fit his modus operandi. However, most historians agree that George "Baby Face" Nelson was among the crooks, and that he was probably the one who did most of the gang's shooting at the bank and during the long car chase that ensued. Incidentally, the thieves got away, in part because they shrewdly forced hostages to ride on the running boards of their Packard getaway car,

America's great love affair with its malls waned, and downtown Sioux Falls had not sunk so far that it couldn't pull itself back up.

making it near impossible for the police to shoot at them. If it was Dillinger, he didn't have much time to spend the loot: the robbery took place on March 6, 1934; on July 22, 1934, Dillinger was shot dead outside a Chicago movie theater.

Just up the street from the Security Bank Building—west, at Ninth Street and Dakota Avenue—is City Hall, a peculiar but peculiarly interesting Art

Deco building that went up in 1936 as a Works Progress Administration (WPA) project. Believe it or not, this low-roofed sand-colored building is Sioux Falls' original City Hall. In the early days of the town, the city rented space in several office buildings scattered around downtown; later they were consolidated into the old City Auditorium, which stood on the site of the present City Hall. If old photos are any guide, the

City Auditorium was a pretty spiffy looking building, but the best thing about it is the story of how it came to exist. In 1898, it seems, the Business Men's League of Sioux Falls managed to snare the 1899 National Butter Makers Association convention. Quite a coup, no doubt, and the businessmen in question were probably so pleased at their success that they didn't immediately realize there was no place in town big

MIKE ROEMER

St. Joseph Cathedral, seat of the Catholic Church here and anchor and namesake of the oldest historic district. Pettigrew, Brookings, McClellan, and other founders of the community lived in the shadow of this French and German Romanesque cathedral—although it was built after most of the notables' homes.

48

Inside St. Joseph Cathedral, the third Catholic church built in the city. The first, a frame structure, burned down in 1881. In 1882, a brick church, St. Michael's Pro-Cathedral, was built on the site of the present cathedral, which was begun in 1915.

enough to hold the assembled butter-makers. Necessity being the mother of special elections, they quickly got the residents to approve an expenditure of nine grand to build an auditorium which would not only have sufficient space for the butter-makers—the City Auditorium seated about 1,000—but also would have room for city offices and the fire department.

Backtrack now, east on Ninth to Phillips Avenue. See what I mean about this being a financial center? There's Norwest Bank on the northwest corner, Western Bank on the northeast

corner, First National Bank on the southeast corner in a building that also houses Merrill Lynch and Dain Bosworth, and Western Surety on the southwest corner. Impressive, sure, but except for the Western Bank Building, which went up in 1917 when banks were built to look like banks and not piles of brick and glass, it's hard to get too worked up about them. (Kudos to First National, however, for rescuing the big stone eagle from the top of their old building when they knocked it down to make room for the current joint.)

Despite the "stone canyon" feel of this intersection, Ninth and Phillips is frequently termed the "most historic corner" in Sioux Falls—and not merely because our absurd street-numbering system emanates from here. This has always been a busy corner. Before Ezra Millard and his cronies packed their bags for the trip up here from Sioux City, Indian trails crossed at what is now Ninth and Phillips. Later, the stagecoaches started from and terminated here, when the Cataract Hotel, the original of which was built in

Fawick Park is named for inventor Thomas Fawick, who built his Fawick Flyer—reputed to be America's first four-door automobile—in his Sioux Falls shop. Shown here is Dr. Rush Brown in the Fawick "Silent Sioux."

1871, was the toniest place in town. Today, the corner is the honorary launching point for Sioux Falls' annual St. Patrick's Day parade, when, at noon on the appointed day, a collection of local political and civic leaders paint an enormous shamrock on the pavement. Rain or shine or, as frequently is the case at that time of year in this part of the country, snow.

There's a lot else to see downtown, of course, if you're of a sightseeing bent, or a historical bent, or both. If we wander on up Phillips Avenue, southward, we'll see plenty of old buildings that have been gussied up and put back into

harness as retail or office space—the building between Tenth and Eleventh, for instance, which now houses Zandbroz Variety; or the restored Shriver-Johnson Building, on Phillips at Eleventh, which previously housed one of the finest department stores in the region and which more recently has been restored and converted to a retail and office center. Fact is, we could pause at nearly every building and say, "Looky—isn't that pretty? Such-and-such used to be there, or so-and-so did this-or-that there." But you can do that anywhere, in any city. And, frankly, there are several nice

guides to and maps of downtown Sioux Falls' historic and architectural attractions. So we'll toddle along—after I point out just a couple more points:

• Phillips Avenue between Eighth and Seventh Streets, designated as the site of Fort Dakota, although the fort covered the equivalent of nearly two blocks.

• The old Federal Building (which some longtime residents still call the new Federal Building, on account of it replaced an even older Federal Building) at Phillips and Twelfth. It was built in chunks in 1895, 1911, and 1935—photographs in the lobby show

how it looked at various stages over the years—and recently restored to its early beauty.

• The old Washington Senior High School, a block west, at Twelfth Street and Main Avenue. Almost a full city block's worth of Sioux Falls Granite, four stories in height, which also was built in stages (1906, 1922, and 1934), and which closed as a school only two years ago. This grand old building's future was in doubt until voters approved a plan to renovate and add to the building, turning it into the Washington Pavilion of Arts and Sciences, to open in 1996. (You see, we do have an increasing appreciation of our own heritage—although it must be pointed out that not every resident thinks the building is worth saving.)

• Finally, no visit to downtown Sioux Falls would be complete without a stop at the tiny, easily overlooked Fawick Park, on Second Avenue between Tenth and Eleventh Streets. Thomas Fawick, a native of Sioux Falls, made his fortune as an inventor and entrepreneur. Indeed, he made his first significant invention, the Four Door Fawick Flyer— an automobile, advertised as America's first four-door—in a shop that still stands on West Thirteenth Street.

Although he left Sioux Falls in 1914, he came back in 1972 and donated to the city one of the only two castings ever made of Michelangelo's sculpture, "David." Interestingly—and strangely—this created a controversy, one that has never really ended, although the diatribes have died down. You see, Michelangelo saw fit to render David *au naturel*, and there was an extremely vocal element at the time who felt that putting a statue—a very large statue, too—of a naked young man on public display would invite all sorts of wickedness upon the city. References to Sodom and Gomorrah were made, despite the fact that neither city had the statue. There was talk—serious talk—of clothing the statue. Or refusing the gift. Or accepting the gift, but hiding it somewhere. In the end, a sort of compromise was reached: the statue went up, in its original state of dishabille, and in a newly created park dedicated to Fawick. But it was set with David's back to the street, and trees were planted to hide the work from motorists crossing the Eleventh Street viaduct. (Undaunted, Fawick subsequently donated a copy of Michelangelo's "Moses," which sits clothed in robes but not con-

troversy on the campus of Augustana College.)

Buildings are only buildings, of course. What's important about downtown Sioux Falls— what may in fact be unique, or certainly unusual, about downtown Sioux Falls—is that there's no shorthand way to sum it up. Retail center? Well, yes, certainly, there's a lot of that, although not as much as there was in those halcyon days before the malling of America. Office center? Well, yes, of course, loads of offices downtown; but then there are office buildings, office complexes tucked away here and there all over town. Financial center? Well, yes, we've mentioned the big stone edifices at Ninth and Phillips; but again, there are others scattered across the city, and the largest single financial entity, Citibank, is *not* located downtown.

So the bottom line, apparently, is that downtown Sioux Falls is eclectic—a hamburger joint sits next to a boutique, which is across the street from a national brokerage firm, which is next to a used-book store, down the block from a three-star restaurant, across from an abandoned movie theater and next to the corporate headquarters of a local retail company, down the street from the federal courthouse,

There's a lot else to see downtown, of course, if you're of a sightseeing bent, or a historical bent, or both.

which sits across from an apartment building, near a television and radio station. And so on. With the single exception of that one big-money intersection at Ninth and Phillips, there's no "row" or enclave of any one sort of business at any given point in downtown Sioux Falls. Eclectic, you might say. Or diverse. Disorganized? All right, if you like: I don't think too many of my fellow residents would wail too long and hard about that description. In fact, I suspect we *like* the diversity reflected in our downtown blocks, or would if we thought much about it, and if it looks disorganized to someone who doesn't live with it, hasn't grown and evolved with it, doesn't see and appreciate it as a reflection of our not-too-distant and still-unfolding history, well, so it goes. Our dedication to the "pioneer spirit," to "rugged individualism," would probably cause us to distrust a downtown district that was *too* slick, too uniform, too unvary-ing. And it would almost certainly cause us to worry very little about what anyone else thought of it.

Take it or leave it, downtown Sioux Falls is what it is—alive, vigorous, growing. In a sense, a snapshot of our past and a blueprint of our future.

The North End

We'll stroll a bit west and slightly north of downtown Sioux Falls now, and take in a neighborhood known locally,

and fondly, as the North End. It's one of the oldest neighborhoods in town—indeed, to the extent that a downtown district probably isn't a "neighborhood" in the usual sense of the word, the North End might be considered Sioux Falls' oldest neighborhood. The North End is usually thought of as running from Russell Street on the north to Tenth Street on the south, and east to west from Main Avenue to West Avenue, a large tract of land which includes the Cathedral Historic District.

This historic district derives its name from the neighborhood's greatest landmark—one of the great landmarks of the

Above: The annual Fourth of July Parade—no, just kidding: the winters don't last that long…but snowy scenes such as this, along Minnesota Avenue, are not an uncommon sight between November and April.
Left: Work crews, construction crews, and everybody else learns to adapt to the sometimes-harsh winters. Perhaps it's the price we pay for usually gorgeous springs and summers.

53

Along about the turn of the 20th century, Minnehaha Springs opened a public bath, offering "spring water baths," "electric baths," "medical lake baths," "tonic baths," and "salt rubs."

entire city, in fact—St. Joseph Cathedral, seat of the Catholic Church in Sioux Falls. Catholicism came relatively late to Sioux Falls, whose good German and Scandinavian settlers established a firm Lutheran tradition that characterizes the city to this day. It wasn't until 1877 that regular Catholic masses were said here, and even then they were celebrated by a "circuit riding" priest. St. Joseph wasn't begun until well into the 20th century, being completed only in 1917. But despite being a relative "new kid" in this old neighborhood, the twin spires of this French and German Romanesque cathedral pretty well symbolize the neighborhood.

Here on the North End, and especially in the 24-square-block historic district south of the Cathedral, lived many of the people whose names are inseparably linked with the early community: W.W. Brookings, one of the early agents of the Western Town Company, who later became Minnehaha County district attorney and eventually a judge, lived at 720 West 4th Street; John McClellan, another of the Western Town Company bunch, who was involved in real estate, newspapering, and banking, lived on the northeast corner of Sixth Street and Minnesota Avenue; R.F. Pettigrew, one of the founders of the "second" Sioux Falls, a philanthropist

and political giant, willed his castle-like quartzite house at Eighth Street and Duluth Avenue to the city to create the Pettigrew Museum; and dozens more. A stroll down virtually any street in this district will reveal this or that architectural gem. I especially recommend Ninth Street between Spring and Prairie Avenues, Eighth Street between the same avenues, and Duluth Avenue between Ninth Street and Fifth Street.

As recently as fifteen or twenty years ago, many of these gems were in serious need of polishing. Many of the houses were still in use as single-family dwellings, and most of those were in good repair, but there were plenty of others that had been pressed into service as low-rent apartments and allowed to take that long grim slide toward decay. But in the mid-1970s, Sioux Falls' nascent sense of the importance of these buildings—with a little help from Congress, which created the National Register of Historic Buildings and Places, and, more significantly, created tax breaks for sites placed on the Register—quite literally rescued them from oblivion. A veritable whirlwind of restoration has been the order of the day since then, to the point where, today, virtually all of these homes, whether grand or more modest, reflect the time when this district was referred to as "Nob Hill" in allusion to all of the fine houses.

But of course the Cathedral District is only a small part of the North End, and most of the homes to the north of the Cathedral are of a more modest mien. This part of the North End was originally built by stone cutters, plumbers, carpenters, blacksmiths, and the others who worked at the quarries, or the brewery, or in downtown businesses. A little rough-and-tumble, perhaps, but the North End was a good, solid working-class neighborhood—as it pretty much is today.

Another North End landmark once stood directly east of the Cathedral, on Spring Avenue. The *appropriately named* Spring Avenue, in fact, since a natural spring runs beneath this entire hilltop neighborhood. (The bishops' tomb beneath St. Joseph Cathedral has never been used, presumably because no one cared to send the bishops to a watery grave.) In 1882 the Heynsohn brothers—presumably they had given names, but you hear them referred to only as the Heynsohn brothers—founded the Sioux Falls Bottling Works at Fourth Street and Spring, bottling not only the spring water but also soda pop and beer from the nearby brewery. More significantly, though, the brothers also built a little park or spa near the works, Minnehaha Springs, which boasted walking paths, flower gardens, and of course a fountain. Along about the turn of the 20th century, Minnehaha Springs opened a public bath, offering "spring water baths," "electric baths," "medical lake baths," "tonic baths," and "salt rubs." The spa was a popular attraction for many years. Today it's all long gone, but the old Minnehaha Springs building is incorporated into and serves as the office of Hawthorne Elementary School.

Hawthorne School, incidentally, is itself a kind of North End landmark, too. The original Hawthorne School was built in 1882, replaced with a new Hawthorne School on the same site in 1924, and replaced yet again with yet another new Hawthorne School in 1985. What persistence! And what a good emblem to stand for this neighborhood.

The All Saints Neighborhood

Our peregrinations take us now south of the business district and into two adjacent neighborhoods that are frequently spoken of in one breath, those surrounding McKennan Park and the former All Saints School. The All Saints neighborhood lies between Minnesota and Sixth Avenues, and Twelfth and Eighteenth Streets. The McKennan neighborhood is usually thought of as being bounded by Eighteenth Street on the north and Twenty-sixth Street on the south, and Minnesota Avenue on the west and Fourth Avenue on the east. Both are listed on the National Register of Historic Places, and both of them have always been and are to this day residential districts, among the most desirable in Sioux Falls.

The All Saints district, un-

Above: *"Sea Dreams," by sculptor and Augusta College professor Steve Thomas, sits downtown near the site of Fort Sod, the first fortification built in Sioux Falls (1858).*
Left: *In the late 1970s and early 1980s, the city began to emerge as a regional financial center. The Midland National Life building's reflective-glass façade is one of the physical manifestations of that reality.*

Facing page: *The Big Sioux River winds its way toward downtown Sioux Falls. You can just see the spires of St. Joseph Cathedral, directly above the bridge over the river.*

57

surprisingly, is dominated by All Saints School, a sprawling, somewhat overblown collection of buildings that perch on a five-acre knoll between Seventeenth and Eighteenth Streets and Phillips and Dakota Avenues. The former Episcopalian school closed, sadly, several years ago, and none of the subsequent plans to make use of the buildings—some of which are more than a century old—have panned out.

The school came to be at the insistence of Episcopalian

opened for business in 1885. Other additions to the campus were made over the years, and All Saints School continued to operate for more than a century, albeit coeducationally in later years.

The establishment of the school encouraged the development of the surrounding neighborhood, and before long the All Saints district was one of the most fashionable in the still-young city. W.L. Dow—Wallace, I think we can call him by now; why did everyone

are still standing, still residences, and still faithful to Dow's originals. (Dow lived in the duplex until his death in 1911; his son lived there until *his* death in 1956; at last check, the house was still in the family.)

As long as we're on First Avenue, we might as well pop down to the next block for a peek at the house that was one of the town's first hospitals, Dunbar Hospital, which operated out of the two-and-a-half-story house at 601 South First Avenue, near Fourteenth Street. Since our shoes haven't begun to pinch, we'll hop across Fourteenth Street and over to Minnesota Avenue, the busy five-lane traffic artery that today is a noisy, malodorous eyesore but which, sixty, eighty, a hundred years ago, was *the* street to live on. Just a couple of doors south of Fourteenth, at 514 South Minnesota, is the only marble house known to have ever existed in Sioux Falls. This pearly gray rather sepulchral building was built in 1907 by Levi W. Ballard, one of the owners of a monument company. Over the past 87 years it has been subjected to an unfortunate concrete-block addition, the strange disappearance of half a story (it used to be two and a half sto-

---

These early residential neighborhoods are like the downtown district—a disorganized patchwork, if you want to look at it that way, or an exciting and intriguing visual record of the growth of the city, if you want to look at it that way.

Bishop William H. Hare, who thought (probably rightly) that the region needed an educational facility for young women. He got the city to donate the site and $10,000, and enlisted our old friend W.L. Dow to design the original school building, in the Venetian fashion. It was built of that familiar Sioux Falls Granite, and

use only initials a hundred years ago?—spent virtually his entire life in Sioux Falls living in this neighborhood. The two houses he built for himself—the first one a two-story Queen Anne he built in 1885 at 700 South First Avenue, and the second one a Tudor duplex he built right next door at 704, in 1895, to share with his son—

Bustling Sioux Falls in 1890.

ries), and a conversion to commercial occupancy. But it's still a heckuva conversation piece.

As we amble back southward, toward All Saints School, and eastward a couple of blocks, into the McKennan neighborhood, it's interesting to note how this neighborhood "grew in" from two directions. For the most part, of course, Sioux Falls spread out from the downtown district. But when the All Saints and McKennan neighborhoods became fashionable, in the late 1880s, homes were built "out there," ten or twenty blocks from the heart of downtown. The territory in between? Fields, mostly, although a certain amount of industry took place in what was probably considered this "outlying" area—a number of brickyards, for instance, operated on what is today the eastern edge of the McKennan neighborhood, and the Pankow Brothers Foundry was in business on Second Avenue from 1884 until 1926. The residences filled in by fits and starts, so that today it's not unusual for an 80- or 90-year-old house to sit across the street from or even next to a house built after the Second World War, with both houses being the first and

only ever built on their respective lots. (Incidentally, the wacky house-numbering system we talked about before gets bogged down here too: the house numbers along Third Avenue, for instance, jump from the 700s to the 900s, right in the middle of the block, for no other reason than that the numbers didn't match up properly when the neighborhoods grew together.) In that respect, these early residential neighborhoods are like the downtown district—a disorganized patchwork, if you want to look at it that way, or an exciting and intriguing visual record of the growth of the city, if you want to look at it *that* way.

Take your pick; you probably already know how I'll vote.

McKennan Park

The future McKennan neighborhood began in 1883, when

Melvin Grigsby and Helen McKennan platted the so-called Boulevard Addition to Sioux Falls. An 1885 advertisement called this "the coming fashionable residence quarter," "one of the pleasantest residence localities in the metropolis of Southern Dakota." And yet it was several years before the neighborhood began to catch on: most of the homes in the McKennan district were built after the turn of the 20th century. Grigsby—a hero of the Civil War and Spanish American War who was active in Sioux Falls politics, banking, law, and real estate (obviously)—built the first house in the neighborhood, at what is now the northwest corner of McKennan Park. Another early resident in the neighborhood was Helen McKennan herself, who subsequently bought Grigsby's house and lived there until her death in 1906. Mrs. McKennan, who was the sister of Artemus Gale, one

of the city's founders, acquired substantial land holdings during her life, and donated much of it upon her death—including the twenty acres that are today known as McKennan Park. Another early resident was E.A. Sherman, a pioneer businessman who is known as the "father of the Sioux Falls park system" on account of his evidently tireless efforts to es-

tablish public parks. Indeed, it was Sherman who arranged for Mrs. McKennan to donate her estate to the city for use as a city park.

That park—McKennan Park—opened in 1908, and is still today the centerpiece of the neighborhood. It stretches from Twenty-first Street on the north—"the Boulevard," as we of the neighborhood call

it—to Twenty-sixth Street on the south, from Second Avenue on the west to Fourth Avenue on the east. McKennan Park has undergone many transformations from its early days. At various points over the decades, McKennan Park has boasted of flower gardens; a small lake; the first public baseball diamond in Sioux Falls; a zoo (two ostriches,

Above: *The seasons are distinct and definite in our city. Here, autumn comes to McKennan Park.*
Right: *Fawick Park is home to one of only two castings ever made of Michelangelo's "David." Since young David is unclothed, the sculpture generated much controversy when Thomas Fawick gave it to the city in 1972.*

Facing page: *Calvary Episcopal Cathedral in downtown Sioux Falls was built in 1888 when Bishop William H. Hare persuaded John Jacob Astor to underwrite the project in honor of Astor's deceased wife.*

two deer, four wolves, three opossum, five pheasants, thirty ducks, one pelican, one monkey, one parrot, two eagles, and two phoenix fowl, according to a 1915 park inventory record); a reflecting pool; a miniature representation of the City of Sioux Falls; a replica of the Statue of Liberty; and the Pillars of the Nation, which bear indigenous rocks, fossils, or other natural artifacts from each of the then-forty-eight states. Today, Sioux Falls residents make

---

The whole blasted neighborhood's filled with houses of historic significance, architectural interest, or just plain good looks.

---

use of the park's tennis courts, ball field, horseshoe court, children's wading pool, children's playground, and ample picnic areas. In the summer there are frequent Sunday-afternoon concerts, courtesy of the Sioux Falls Municipal Band; in the winter the Parks Department floods the ball field and plays ice-skating music over the P.A. The Pillars of the Nation are still there, on the Second Avenue side, and some of the arti-

facts haven't yet been pried out by vandals.

Because it took awhile for this neighborhood to become trendy, most of the houses here were built after the turn of the 20th century. Until 1917, in fact, the land east of the park, from Fourth Avenue to about Seventh Avenue, was a nine-hole golf course. As late as 1910, "Cattle grazed on the open area adjoining the scattered homes and lawns. Prairie chickens were so plentiful in the summer and fall that an en-

ergetic boy with a sharp shooting eye and a trusty gun could bag enough of these game birds for mama to serve the family at supper," according to my friend Delores Harrington in her book *The McKennan Hospital Story*. The oldest standing house in the neighborhood was built by Edward Coughran, a Sioux Falls real estate agent, at 1203 South First Avenue. It's a gorgeous old Queen Anne, either well-maintained or well-restored, whose most impressive features are

the three huge brick chimneys that stand watch over the peaks of the roof.

The problem with this neighborhood is that no matter which direction you set out from the park, you will find, at worst, an interesting-looking old house and, at best, a fabulous-looking old house. The city has published a nice self-directed walking-tour map of the neighborhood, and rather than try to duplicate it, let's just have a peek at some of my favorites. (They're my favorites, incidentally, not because I know much about architecture, but because I either like the house or like the story behind it. Or both.)

• The Lein/Hollister House sits just across from the park, at Second Avenue and the Boulevard. Burre Lein was mayor of Sioux Falls at the turn of the 20th century. He built this grand Italianate house in 1885 and lived here until 1913, at which time F.H. Hollister, of Hollister Brothers Loan Company, purchased it.

• Directly south of the Lein/Hollister House, a Tudor Revival structure built in 1928, by Sioux Grigsby, a local lawyer and the son of Melvin Grigsby. Grigsby lived here until his death in 1976.

• Farther down the block, at Second Avenue and Twenty-fourth Street, is a unique house—unique in Sioux Falls, anyhow—that locals consistently say was built by Frank Lloyd Wright. No. It's a Wright *design* for an Oriental-flavored California bungalow, built in 1915 for Henry C. Fenn, co-owner of the Fenn Brothers Ice Cream and Confectionery Company—as a summer home! (The Fenn Brothers, incidentally, reputedly invented butter brickle ice cream, the fiends.)

• Across from the north side of the park at Third Avenue and the Boulevard, sits a…well, frankly, a peculiar sort of place, Mediterranean in flavor, primarily Italian with certain Spanish overtones as well. You don't get a lot of that sort of thing around these parts. It was built in 1916 for Frank H. Weatherwax, founder of F.H. Weatherwax Clothing, which remained a Sioux Falls staple—and a family-owned enterprise—until closing just a few years ago.

• On the east side of the park, at Fourth Avenue and the Boulevard, is an imposing Tudor Revival structure, built in 1916 for William L. Baker, the president of First National Bank. The house remained in the Baker family's hands for many years, but currently it's owned by *our* family's doctor, so Peg and I like to think that by extension we own a little chunk of it.

And so on—as I say, the whole blasted neighborhood's filled with houses of historic significance, architectural interest, or just plain good looks. Wander up or down almost any block, and enjoy.

Although it's technically outside of the neighborhood, as the neighborhood is usually defined, it's tough to talk about the McKennan district without mentioning McKennan Hospital, which sprawls across several acres beginning at Seventh Avenue and Twentieth Street. Helen McKennan's will not only donated the land for McKennan Park, but also included $25,000 to found a hospital. At that time—1906, when Mrs. McKennan died—the Catholic church was exploring the possibility of creating a new hospital for the growing community. The bequest provided the means, and McKennan Hospital opened its doors in 1911. Today, like any other major medical facility, McKennan Hospital seems to be in a perpetual and permanent state of construction and expansion, yet somehow it remains a neighborhood facility.

We have wandered through some of the oldest neighborhoods in town—naturally enough, I suppose. But that may leave you with the impression that, contrary to the assertion I made some pages back, Sioux Falls is an "old" city. Not so. In the last twenty years, and especially in the last ten years, the town has sprawled—there's no other word for it: it has *sprawled*—to the east, the southeast, and the southwest, so that, acre for acre, there's certainly more "new Sioux Falls" than "old Sioux Falls." I learned how to drive in this town, and yet I increasingly find myself coming upon street names that are totally unfamiliar to me; I don't even know what *end* of town they're on, let alone how to get to them! And there's no end in sight: Urban planners anticipate the population of metropolitan Sioux Falls alone increasing two percent a year for the foreseeable future. That may not seem like much—two measly percent—but with a current population of about 110,000, two percent equals 2,200 people. If that two percent holds, you're looking at about 112,200 people in 1995; roughly 125,000 by the end of the 20th century. A young city indeed! And a city busily building new neighborhoods with their own distinct personalities and attributes.

A
Sioux
Falls
Album

Above: *Downtown, looking southeast. Just behind Norwest is the Security Bank Building, robbed in 1934—of nearly $46,000—by bandits reputed to have been part of Dillinger's gang.*

Facing page, top: *Every August, the Sioux Empire Fair is held at the W.H. Lyon Fairgrounds in the western part of town—as every kid for miles around knows!*

Bottom: *The McKennan Park district has long been one of the favorite residential neighborhoods in the city. (But much of it was a nine-hole golf course until 1917!)*

Above: *The Big Sioux isn't the only water around: there are numerous natural and man-made lakes in the area, not to mention the Missouri River.*

Left: *A local artist finds just the right landscape for her canvas.*

Facing page: *Among the many annual events in and around the city is the Great Plains Balloon Race, held in June.*

Many early entrepreneurs sought to harness the energy of the Falls, and failed. Today, as in the days of Nicollet, the Falls are a thing of beauty, not a slave of commerce.

Right: This sandhill crane is among the nearly 250 animals of more than 70 species at home in the Great Plains Zoo. The Zoo features the Children's Zoo and the Penguin Pool, with the African Savannah currently under construction. The facility also houses the Delbridge Museum of Natural History.

Below: As early as A.D. 800, agriculture was important to the area. It's nice to know some things never change!

Above: *The waters of the Big Sioux River are deceptive: They seem almost lazy, but here you can see they're more energetic than a casual glance may reveal.*

Left: *Despite the Queen City's abundance of parks, some–times a quiet residential street is the best playground!*

DANIEL R. JENSEN

Leisure

DANIEL R. JENSEN

On any given weekend, any of the city's parks may offer an informal musical presentation or other bit of entertainment.

NATURAL ATTRACTIONS.
Not only has "Dame Nature" been kind to Sioux Falls in supplying the city with multitudinous resources which may be transmuted into dollars, but she has likewise favored her with more than a due share of attractions which appeal to the aesthetic instincts of those who behold them. The scenery of the vicinity is beautiful. The general contour of the country is such a commingling of slope and valley and plain as gives infinite variety. The river meanders in the form of a gigantic S, astride the middle strand of which the city stands....

—E.W. CALDWELL
SIOUX FALLS ILLUSTRATED, *1888*

Every so often, you hear it. As a matter of fact, *pretty* often you hear it, and it goes like this: "There's nothing to do around here." (For maximum effect, it should be delivered in a whine.) And it gets repeated so often that it takes on the patina of truth, and no one responds, as would be proper to do: "What on *earth* are you talking about?!"

Because the truth is, there's loads of stuff to do around here.

Of course, it comes down in part by what you mean by "stuff to do." Night clubs? Not really. Performance art? Sorry. Planetarium? Yeah, right. And of course we've already established that the tallest building in town is only eleven stories, so that pretty much rules out riding up to some cloud-level observation platform and watching the dirigibles come in. You also, as long as we're on the subject, can't go deep-sea diving anywhere in Sioux Falls, nor are there any nearby mountains to climb (although the Minnesota Avenue hill is

Water sports are wildly popular—perhaps because our season for them is relatively short.

In addition to the leisure-activity opportunities in the city proper, there's an almost infinite number of recreational facilities within a brief drive—for instance, Lewis & Clark Recreation Area, on the Missouri River near Yankton, about 80 miles southwest.

pretty steep), and surfing is right out.

But contrary to popular opinion—popular, that is, amongst high-school students and certain others who don't know any better but probably should—there's plenty to do in and around Sioux Falls.

Culturally, virtually any night of the week—any season of the year—offers something. The South Dakota Symphony, based in Sioux Falls, plays a full season of concerts and frequently brings in guest performers: in the past year or two Ray Charles, Bobby McFerrin, and the Moody Blues have performed with the Symphony. The Dakota String Quartet and the Dakota Woodwind Quintet appear regularly in concert. Every year, the Community Concert Association imports four or five performers and performances from around the world. There are several choral groups, including the Sioux Falls Master Singers and the Singing Boys of Sioux Falls, as well as concerts, recitals, and other musical events from the local colleges and high schools. And the Friends of Traditional Music sponsors all kinds of events—Irish music, bluegrass music, folk music, and more—at various times and places throughout the year.

Major and—let's be honest—once-major popular acts frequently perform in Sioux Falls: Barry Manilow, Kenny Rogers, Vince Gill, and Aerosmith have graced the stage of the Sioux Falls Arena within recent memory; the Glenn Miller Orchestra usually comes through once or twice a year; and the annual Sioux Empire Fair always includes a long list of current favorites, usually from the country charts, as well as heavy schedule of "nostalgia acts" that may not make the charts anymore but still seem perfectly capable of pleasing a crowd. We won't even talk about all the local performers and bands that are playing all the time at the Pomp Room, or the back room at Zandbroz Variety, or Teddy's

Mediterranean & American Cafe and Pub, or the Westroads Lounge, or—well, you get the picture.

Not into music? How about theater? The Sioux Falls Community Playhouse mounts several local productions every season. The Sioux Empire Entertainment League brings national touring companies of Broadway shows into the Coliseum four or five times a year. Augustana College and Sioux Falls College are forever staging productions, as are the high-school drama departments.

And if you don't mind a short drive—to Tea, South Dakota, for instance, just south of the city, or Worthing, South Dakota, fifteen miles farther south, you can take in one of the regular performances at the Barn Theater or the Olde Town Theatre. (Shoot, if you don't mind a little drive, there are at least half a dozen colleges and universities within a seventy-five or eighty-mile radius of Sioux Falls, any of which is presenting a play, recital, concert, or other entertainment event at any given time.)

You like museums, galleries, that sort of thing? Okay. The Siouxland Heritage Museums oversees two, which we've already mentioned: the Old Courthouse Museum, located in the original Minnehaha County Courthouse building at Fifth and Main downtown; and the Pettigrew Home and Museum, located in the former home of R.F. Pettigrew, one of the city's founders, boosters, and political giants. The latter is dedicated more to the early history of this region and community, while the former deals not only with that but also treats more contemporary subjects and hosts traveling exhibitions.

Downtown you'll also find the Civic Fine Arts Center, located in the old Carnegie Public Library building at Tenth and Dakota, which presents a crowded calendar of exhibits by local as well as national and international artists; and the Northern Plains Gallery at Sixth and Phillips, which displays Native American works, especially those by artists of the Northern Plains tribes—which is quite a different kettle of fish from the Southwestern tribal art many people think of when they hear the words "Native American art." At Augustana College, there's

Professionals—the Sioux Falls Skyforce, of the Continental Basketball Association. "The Force" is the developmental team of the Minnesota Timberwolves.

the Center for Western Studies, which focuses on current times as well as past history of this part of the country, as well as the Eide/Dalrymple Gallery, which displays student and professional creations. At Sioux Falls College, there's almost always a display or exhibit at the Norman B. Mears Library. And of course there are any number of private galleries which sell art as well as display it.

A rather peculiar—and not to be missed—addition to the list of Sioux Falls museums and galleries is the Delbridge Museum of Natural History, which is adjacent to the Great Plains Zoo on Kiwanis Avenue near Twelfth Street. In a manner of speaking the Delbridge Museum had its beginnings in a store called West Sioux Hardware, which closed in 1981. The store's owner, Henry Brockhouse, was interested in far more than pipe fittings and paint thinner. He was an honest-to-goodness big-game hunter, and he must have been fairly good at it, too, because his store boasted an impressive (and, to a ten-year-old kid, rather spooky: I speak from experience again) collection of mounted rhinos, bears, elephants, and cats bigger than the one who likes to snooze on

Water sports are certainly popular, but so are a few dry-land games. There are two municipal golf courses and two privately owned public courses, and three private country-club courses.

77

Above: The Sioux Falls Canaries, of the Northern League, is the Queen City's professional baseball team. The team is the spiritual, albeit not literal, descendant of the original Canaries, who played from the late 1890s through the early 1930s and again from the late '30s through 1952.

Facing page, top: Money magazine, in naming Sioux Falls the "Best Place to Live in America," gave the city low scores on the arts—but art is where you find it!

Bottom: The U.S.S. South Dakota was the most decorated battleship of World War II; the U.S.S. Battleship South Dakota Memorial, in the Sherman Park Complex, features examples of the ship's equipment and appointments.

my computer monitor while I work. Following Brockhouse's death, in 1978, and the store's closing, in 1981, the fate of his menagerie—reputed to be the largest privately owned such collection in the world—was uncertain. Then the C.J. Delbridge family bought the collection and donated it to the city, provided that the city build a suitable facility for displaying the animals. The result, 16,000 square feet later, is the Delbridge Museum of Natural History, home to Brockhouse's 175-animal collection—although the museum features exhibits, displays, and educational shows in addition to the Brockhouse animals.

In the same complex, of course, is the Great Plains Zoo, one of the city's top attractions for more than thirty years. At the moment almost 250 animals representing more than 70 species call the zoo home, but almost certainly those numbers will have increased by the time you read these words. The Great Plains Zoo seems always to be growing, always expanding. In fact, the zoo is a good example of what we were talking about at the beginning of this book, that "deceptively active" nature of Sioux Falls.

I said then that there's always a lot going on in this city, even if you're not aware of it.

That's definitely true of the Great Plains Zoo. When I was a kid in Sioux Falls, say, twenty-five years ago, the zoo was…well, a zoo. A bunch of cramped cages in which a bunch of animals lounged around, bored, on slabs of concrete. (Except for the mountain goats: I always remember the mountain goats being out in the open on their ersatz mountain made of—you guessed it—Sioux Falls Granite.) Today there's one very small portion of the facility that's still like that, but its days are numbered. Most of the animals now are out in the open, in spacious surroundings carefully crafted to resemble their natural habitat. There's the Children's Zoo and the Penguin Pool. An African savanna is currently under construction, and when it's completed the big cats will be out from behind bars, and the last of the old zoo will be gone for good and for the better. But there's never been any big to-do about it, no big brouhaha, no let's-fix-up-the-zoo campaign. It's just sort of been taking place, quietly, behind the scenes, day by day, until one day you happen to wander in there and think to yourself, "Hey, this is a pretty neat zoo."

• • •

The pretty neat zoo is part of the city's Sherman Park Complex, which sprawls along the Big Sioux River from Twelfth Street to Twenty-Second Street and which includes two playground areas, picnic sites galore, a multi-diamond baseball facility, and a memorial to the *U.S.S. South Dakota*, the most decorated battleship of World War II. The ship itself is not here, of course, just pieces of it, including a Tiffany silver service that was presented to the *South Dakota*'s captain when the ship was commissioned in 1942. But until last year, Sherman Park also contained Dennis the Menace Park, in which kids

79

This page: Locally, the first average freeze date is October 1 and the last average freeze date is May 10. So, you may rightly guess that winter activities, and activities adapted to wintertime, are big around here!

Facing page: The Sioux Falls Community Playhouse, which is at home here in the old Orpheum Theatre, mounts several local productions every season: the Sioux Empire Entertainment League brings national touring companies to town.

who had progressed beyond swing sets and jungle gyms could play on and in an actual bomber, an anti-aircraft gun, a tank, a fire engine…all non-working, unfortunately. Alas, Dennis the Menace Park has fallen victim to the growing zoo's need for real estate, and, one suspects, political correctness.

On the subject of parks: this town is lousy with them. Sioux Falls has got to be one of the most park-happy communities in the world. Currently, the Parks and Recreation Department is responsible for 64 city parks, which take up almost 1,800 acres. The whole city covers about 50 square miles. Math was never my strong suit,

but I work that out to be better than five percent of the city's land dedicated to public parks. Some of these parks are quite small, the sort that in other communities might be called "vest pocket parks"—Van Eps Park, for instance, sometimes dubbed a "rest park," at Seventh and Minnesota. Others are quite extensive—McKen-

City Auditorium—later the site of City Hall—was built through the efforts of the Business Men's League of Sioux Falls in 1898 when the group snared the 1899 National Butter Makers Association convention and then realized there was no place in town large enough to host such an event.

nan Park, as we've already seen, or Sherman Park. Many of the city's parks have tennis courts and swimming pools; nearly all have, at a minimum, playground equipment and picnic facilities. Terrace Park, adjacent to Covell Lake on the very north end of the North End, has its beautiful Shototeien Japanese Tea Gardens; Tuthill Park, in an upscale neighborhood on the south end of town, has a glorious long hill on which, every winter, untold numbers of adolescents lose untold square inches of skin in death-defying sledding and tobogganing escapades. Each park has its own features, its own personality. And even as we've been talking about them, the city has probably added two or three more parks to the list.

So it shouldn't shock you too much to learn that, recreationally speaking, Sioux Falls is a very outdoorsy community. We swim, we golf, we ski, we boat, we fish, we hunt, we skate, we play softball like nobody's business. And we don't much care what season of the year it is either. In the winter, our ever-active friends at Parks and Rec operate nine public ice-skating rinks and three cross-country ski trails. Last year the city purchased Great Bear Ski Valley, previously a privately owned downhill-skiing facility just northeast of town, putting that sport within the reach of more residents. (Yes, we have hills high enough for downhill skiing even in South Dakota. As I said before, the land here is *pretty* flat, not *completely* flat. Still, honesty compels me to

Daytripping

Honesty requires our noting that not everything of interest takes place within the Sioux Falls city limits. As alluded to elsewhere, there's lots going on *around* Sioux Falls virtually all the time. People in Sioux Falls think nothing of hopping in the car and driving 237 miles to Minneapolis or 184 miles to Omaha or even 750 miles to Denver for a weekend of shopping, theater-going, or plain old hanging around. But you don't have to drive hundreds of miles to find something to do. For instance:

• Newton Hills State Park, located south of Canton, which in turn is 23 miles southeast of Sioux Falls, is a wonderful nature area for campers, hikers, horseback riders, and just about anyone else.

• Lewis & Clark Recreation Area is located in Yankton, 80 miles southwest of Sioux Falls. Camping, boating (on Lewis & Clark Lake, formed by the Gavins Point Dam on the Missouri River), water sports, and fishing are the big attractions here. Yankton's early role in the development of Dakota Territory and the State of South Dakota rivals Sioux Falls', and the town is rife with historical sites.

• Palisades State Park, another natural wonder, near Garretson, South Dakota, just northeast of Sioux Falls. The Palisades are composed of that familiar pinkish quartzite known locally as Sioux Falls Granite (and outside the city limits as Sioux Granite), carved and polished by Split Rock Creek. Camping, swimming, canoeing, fishing, hiking, and—you guessed it—rock climbing are big draws here.

• For indoor sports of a different variety, there's casino gambling on many Indian lands throughout the area: Royal River Casino in Flandreau, South Dakota, 35 miles north of Sioux Falls, is one of the better known in the region. Caution: When the gambling bug bit South Dakota a few years ago, every hole-in-the-wall tavern with a single video poker machine in the back hung out a shingle with the magic word *casino* on it. But currently there are no "real" casinos in Sioux Falls proper.

• Finally, Mitchell, South Dakota—about 75 miles west of Sioux Falls on Interstate 90—has a lot to offer: Soukup & Thomas International Balloon and Airship Museum, Enchanted World Doll Museum, Oscar Howe Art Center (Howe was a Sioux Indian artist of worldwide repute), and, of course, the World's Only Corn Palace. This is a curious, vaguely mosque-like auditorium decorated annually with, um, corn. Lots of it, different varieties and different colors, inside and out, arranged to form mosaic-like images and illustrations. And the "world's only" is no mere bit of hype. In the late nineteenth and early twentieth century, corn palaces dotted the Midwestern landscape. One by one they faded, leaving only Mitchell's.

MIKE ROEMER

admit that skiing Great Bear isn't exactly like skiing the Swiss Alps. Not that I've ever skied the Swiss Alps...) Hockey is a favorite here as well, especially youth hockey.

Of course, even *our* winters don't last forever, and when the last of the snow melts along about Independence Day (just kidding), the warm-weather activities kick into high gear. Come spring, the city goes softball crazy. American Legion softball is the big thing, but it seems sometimes that every tavern, every restaurant, every fraternal or civic organization, every *everything* sponsors a softball team for this or that age category.

Tennis and golf are extremely popular in Sioux Falls, too, and have been for as long as I can remember—locally, at least, both seem immune to the "boom and bust" nature of certain sports that are "in" for a season or two, then "out" again. Racquetball seems to have had its heyday in Sioux Falls—there are still racquetball courts, of course, and plenty of racquetball enthusiasts who will no doubt be lying in wait for me for saying that the sport's day seems to have come and gone—but tennis and golf are perennials. Currently there are two municipal golf courses and two privately owned public courses, and constant talk of adding more of each. In addition, the town's two country clubs, the Minnehaha Country Club and the Westward Ho Country Club, have three courses between them.

Am I beginning to convince you that there *are* things to do here?

Sioux Falls is a real "kids' town." Both the city and the YMCA run a more than full schedule of activities for kids from pre-school on up—swimming lessons, day camps, overnight camps, basketball, volleyball, children's theater, youth band, arts and crafts in the park. You would be hard-pressed to name a team sport for which there isn't a local kids' league. If you came up with one—jai alai, for instance; I'm pretty sure there's no youth jai alai in Sioux Falls—you could probably get a league going with only a phone call or two. It's that kind of city.

It's also an "events" kind of city—parades (the annual St. Patrick's Day Parade in March, the annual Parade of Lights in November, the annual Holiday parade in December, plus any number of "ad hoc" parades); shows (the annual Sioux Empire Farm Show in February, the annual Sidewalk Arts Festival in September, the annual Northern Plains Tribal Arts Show and Market, also in September, plus any number of "sports" shows, church and charity shows and sales, etc.); and sporting events (the annual high school basketball tournaments in March, the annual Howard Wood Dakota Relays in May, the annual Great Plains Balloon Race in June). The El Riad Circus comes through every April, and the Sioux Empire Fair is held every August.

Have I mentioned we get something like thirty channels on cable TV, plus half a dozen "premium" channels, plus pay-per-view?

The Queen City also is home to two professional sports teams, the Sioux Falls Skyforce, of the sixteen-team Continental Basketball Association, and the Sioux Falls Canaries, of baseball's independent Northern League. The Skyforce, which is the official developmental team of the Minnesota Timberwolves, plays 28 home games a season; the Canaries play 36 home games a season—and we play baseball *outdoors* around here, in-

cidentally, the way the game was meant to be played. (The Canaries have a long, albeit occasionally interrupted history. The original Sioux Falls Canaries played from the late 1890s until the early 1930s, folded, formed again in the late 1930s, and folded again in 1952. The current team, one of six Northern League teams, was founded in 1992. There was a different Northern League in existence until the early 1970s, and Sioux Falls fielded a team then, too, appropriately if imitatively dubbed the Packers.)

Collegiate and high-school sports—notably, though certainly not exclusively, basketball and football—also figure prominently in this community. And if you like your sports long-distance, nearly everyone in town is a fan of the Minnesota Vikings, the Minnesota Timberwolves, or the Minnesota Twins—or all of the above.

Above: A mild day, a park, a volleyball net—what else is there to say?

Facing page: Self-reliance may be a facet of the local character, but so too is an immediate and expansive response to charity events, relief efforts, and any of dozens of other "good causes."

(I am only half joking when I tell people that Sioux Falls is the most distant suburb of the Twin Cities of Minneapolis and St. Paul.)

Still at loose ends? Well, eat something, you'll feel better—Sioux Falls is slowly becoming a "restaurant town," although fast-food and "family" restaurants seem to fare better than fine-dining establishments. As the population diversifies, so too does the local menu, with Chinese Hunan and Szechwan cuisine—and, less successfully, Japanese and Vietnamese cuisine—taking their place alongside the traditional steaks and chicken. Restaurants are notorious for coming and going, but after more than a decade it seems safe to say that Minerva's, downtown, consistently offers the finest "fine dining" experience in town, as acknowledged by the *Guide Michélin*.

And then there's shopping. As the largest community in its region, Sioux Falls is naturally something of a magnet for shoppers. Annual retail sales exceed $1.0 billion. The city has somewhere in the neighborhood of 800 retailers, servicing about half a million customers. The carpet in the Empire Mall is mashed down by ten to twelve million pairs of feet every year—as some figure it, it's that mall, not Mount Rushmore, which is South Dakota's biggest tourist attraction. Sioux Falls' stores, whether "malled" or not, run the gamut from local to regional to national, and the list of national chains or franchises adding the Queen City to their location sites is always lengthening: just a few weeks ago it was announced that Toys 'R' Us will be opening a Sioux Falls store in time for Christmas 1994; in 1992, The Disney Store pulled a similar just-in-time stunt. Can F.A.O. Schwarz be far behind?

If you are not yet convinced that the "nothing-to-do-around-here" lament is bogus, then I fear there's no hope for you. There's loads of things to do in and around Sioux Falls—perhaps even too much to do, if you're prone to hyperactivity or over-involvement. And we haven't even touched on all the myriad church groups, service organizations, and volunteer organizations that exist here. A word of advice: Pace yourself.

We haven't touched, either, on one of the most splendid recreational facilities in Sioux Falls, the Big Sioux River Recreation Trail and Greenway. More familiarly—though less accurately—called "the Bike Trail," the Greenway is an ambitious project which reflects not only our collective love of the outdoors but also our historical ties to the Big Sioux River. Beginning at Falls Park and following the path of the river (albeit backwards), the Greenway connects a series of bike and pedestrian trails, dikes, and city parks in a lush, well-tended, not-quite-completed circuit of the city. Visible along the trail are many of the plant species indigenous to the prairie, thanks to the river providing "free transportation" for seeds and spores, as well as local animal life, including red squirrels, turtles, ducks, and other birds. The city has provided access points via the various parks along the route, which also make for convenient "rest stops." Whether you bike the entire fifteen completed miles (roughly from Falls Park around the south end of town and up to the airport) or simply stroll along a small stretch of it, the Greenway is a beautiful, serene way to "get away from it all" without ever leaving town, and appreciate the river without which there would be no Falls and, by extension, no Sioux Falls.

Seasons

Old Joke Number One: "There are four seasons here: Winter, winter, winter, and road construction."

Old Joke Number Two: "If you don't like the weather here, stick around: It'll change in a few minutes."

Of course, the reason these tired old jokes got to *be* tired old jokes is that they contain at least a kernel of truth. Yes, the winters in these parts can be long—and hard, which means the road crews have to rush out and try to make all repairs virtually simultaneously as soon as the snow melts. And, yes, especially in the spring and fall the weather can change dramatically day by day, and sometimes even in a single day. On one particular day in the spring, we started out with temperatures in the forties, sunny skies, mild spring breezes. Within a couple of hours, the mercury fell, ominous clouds moved in, the wind kicked up, and snow began lashing the trees. Later that afternoon the wind died down, the sun came back from coffee break, and the snow melted. About the only thing we didn't get that day were tidal waves.

Such meteorological looniness notwithstanding, Sioux Falls occupies a spot on the globe where the seasons are distinct and definite. Winter can be harsh, snowy, and windy. We *are* fairly far north, you know, despite the state being named *South* Dakota, and being on the prairie there aren't a lot of big trees and mountains and such to stop the Arctic winds from racing in from Canada. Spring is usually mild and, well, springlike, although, since we live in a river valley, flash flooding can be a problem after a particularly snowy winter. Summer ordinarily is hot, sunny, and windy, and punctuated with thunderstorms and tornadoes. Autumn is frequently blustery and wet, and occasionally non-existent: it's not entirely unusual to go almost directly from summer to winter, but most years we get to enjoy the leaves turning. (A particularly good way to observe the fall colors is to head for the "bike trail," the Big Sioux River Recreation Trail and Greenway, at almost any point in its meander around the city.)

If you're into climatalogical trivia: The average annual temperature in Sioux Falls is 45 degrees; the average annual wind-speed is 11.1 miles an hour; the number of sunny days is about 237 a year; average precipitation is 24.12 inches; average *frozen* precipitation is 39.8 inches; the first average freeze date is October 1 and the last average freeze date is May 10. It may be worth mentioning, in that regard, that the Great Plains Zoo has to send the penguins on vacation every winter *because it's too blasted cold for them here!* The Siberian tigers, however, like it just fine.

Having never lived anywhere but the Midwest, I'll have to take it on faith when people who have spent time in the Sunbelt say that they really miss the changing seasons. In Sioux Falls, though, you can't *possibly* miss them!

Book-learnin'

DANIEL R. JENSEN

Above: Like kids everywhere else, kids here can't wait for school to let out so they can go off to play—on the school playground.

Facing page: Augustana College (top) and Sioux Falls College (bottom), sponsored respectively by the Evangelical Lutheran Church in America and the American Baptist Churches in the U.S.A., are fully accredited four-year liberal arts colleges and longtime fixtures of the local landscape.

Having already gone on record stating that Sioux Falls is a "kids' town," I shouldn't have to brace you for the news that Sioux Falls is chock-full of schools—most of which are in turn chock-full of kids. Every time you turn around, a new school is under construction somewhere—or being added on to, or being planned. I can think of two under construction right at the moment, with two more on the drawing boards. And who knows how many others the school district has up its collective sleeve, waiting only for the proper moment to spring them on the taxpayers.

Vital statistics: There are more than 17,000 students enrolled in Sioux Falls' public schools. That's more—lots more—than a good many surrounding towns' total populations. This little army is deployed among 23 elementary schools, four middle schools, and three high schools—that's only the ones that are actually open for business, mind, not those under construction or being blueprinted. There are not quite 1,100 public-school teachers in the district.

In addition, there are sixteen private schools, most of them church-affiliated, with enrollments totaling just over 3,000.

On average, roughly half of the city's high-school graduates go on to college; not quite ten percent go into vocational training programs; a few go into the military; the remainder go straight into the workforce. At least for a while.

Meaning what? Meaning that Sioux Falls has become—on top of everything else we've been discussing!—something of a center for "nontraditional" education.

Let's talk first of all about "traditional" higher education ("post-secondary" is the current term for "higher education," handily encompassing just about everything that happens after high school). Sioux Falls has *always* been at least a medium-sized center for

higher education. In the early days of the town's settlement, civic promoters worked tirelessly to attract colleges and universities. Why? Good investment. Colleges meant students, students spent money, students graduated and built houses, and so on. Colleges brought prestige upon a community, and it probably would not be an overstatement to assert that in the late 1800s, darn near *every* stripling community on the prairie wanted one. Or more.

Today Sioux Falls is home to two four-year liberal-arts colleges, primarily—if not exclusively—because of that century-old desire, and because of the community's willingness to put its money where its mouth was. Literally: In 1881, area Baptists were looking around for a place to build a college; Sioux Falls offered them $6,000 and a free building site if they put it here. In 1883, Dakota Collegiate Institute opened for business, and is in business yet today under the name Sioux Falls College. Sioux Falls College offers more than 30 major fields of study to more than 1,000 students.

Six years later, it was the Lutherans who were looking for a college site, and again the citizenry reached for its wallet: residents raised $5,600 cash, and R.F. Pettigrew and his

business partner, Samuel L. Tate, donated the land for the Norwegian Evangelical Lutheran Synod to build its Lutheran Normal Training School here. In 1918, when a merger of churches resulted in a merger of Lutheran Normal School with Augustana College in nearby Canton, South Dakota, the united schools took on the latter's name and the former's location. Now Augustana College is home-away-from-home for about 2,000 students in various undergraduate and master's-degree programs.

Although it's not a college, the South Dakota School for the Deaf was a product of the same era and the same attitude that caused the formation of Augustana College and Sioux Falls College. Known originally as the School for the Deaf and Mute, and built by private backers in 1880, the school was taken over almost immediately by the state, which runs it to this day. The nationally recognized school works with both resident and nonresident deaf and hearing-impaired students from birth through age twenty-one.

We've already mentioned another product of that time and philosophy: All Saints School, built by Bishop William H. Hare of the Episcopal church in 1884, with a gift from the city of $10,000 and land. Originally a school for young women, All Saints School redefined itself several times during its 100-year life.

Sioux Falls has become—on top of everything else we've been discussing!—something of a center for "nontraditional" education.

When it closed in the late 1980s, it was a coeducation grade school.

It probably sounds a little corny, but nevertheless we do owe a debt of gratitude to those early civic leaders who campaigned so vigorously for colleges and schools to be built here. For all of the above-mentioned institutions have benefited not only their students but also the entire community, and continue to do so to this day (excluding, of course, the now-closed All Saints School). Incidentally, it would be unfair to leave you with the impression that those early residents wanted colleges and schools built here only for mercenary reasons. Yes, they were businessmen, most of them, and they undoubtedly saw the great economic rewards a successful college could bring to a young city. But there's also reason to consider those people in a philanthropic light as well, for they dug into their own wallets as readily as they asked their fellow taxpayers to dig into theirs. For instance, the land for the School for the Deaf was donated by our old friend E.A. Sherman, and the original buildings were all designed by our even older friend W.L.. Dow. C.K. Howard, a wealthy merchant—he operated the sutler's store at Fort Dakota, and went on to build several other successful businesses—put up $5,000 to get the venture rolling. That was in 1881. Fewer than twenty years later, Howard was penniless. When he died in 1918, the people of Sioux Falls raised money for a fitting burial and monument: $5,000. As they say, what goes around comes around.

Remember how I cryptically alluded to those high-school graduates who go straight into the workforce "at least for a while?" I alluded also to "non-traditional" students—basically, those who don't follow the typical course of heading straight from high school to college or vocational school—and Sioux Falls has a lot to offer the adult student, the working student, and the retraining student. Kilian Community College—originally founded by Augustana College, Sioux Falls College, and the North American Baptist Seminary (which also is located here, and which offers graduate training in areas related to religion and counseling)—began in 1977 specifically to provide college credit to working adults. The Degree Completion Program at Sioux Falls College has similar aims. Huron University, a private institution based in Huron, South Dakota, offers primarily business-related courses oriented to working adults at its Sioux Falls branch. Similarly, most of the institutions in the state-university system offer certain specific courses through "satellite

centers" in Sioux Falls—for instance, it is possible to earn an MBA degree from the University of South Dakota without traveling the sixty miles to Vermillion—geared primarily to working adults.

There are other educational roads open to both working adults and students right out of high school: Nettleton Junior College, Stenotype Institute of South Dakota, and National College are privately owned schools featuring business-related curricula. Stewart School of Hairstyling trains students for careers in hairstyling and related fields.

Also attracting both traditional and "nontraditional students," in both day and evening courses, is Southeast Technical Institute, a public post-secondary school founded by the state Board of Vocational Education and overseen by the Sioux Falls school district. Southeast began in 1968 with just over 100 students; today it occupies a campus of three buildings—with a fourth under construction—and teaches

nearly ten times the original number of students. And that doesn't include such "extracurricular" activities as business and industry training, special seminars and workshops, and other such programs.

That's all within the Sioux Falls city limits. Within a 60-mile radius of the city, there are at least half a dozen other educational institutions—including South Dakota State University in Brookings, the University of South Dakota in Vermillion, and Dakota State University in Madison (with one of the region's most highly regarded computer science and data processing programs)—for those who don't mind a commute. But it's a safe bet that as the population of Sioux Falls continues to increase, those and other colleges and universities will offer more and more programs in metropolitan Sioux Falls. And we probably won't even have to raise cash tributes to lure them here!

Health Care and High Technology

ROBERT L. KELLEHER

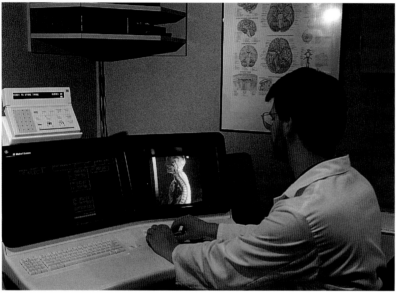

In recent years, Sioux Falls has emerged as a regional medical center, offering facilities, services, and technologies previously found only in Minneapolis, Rochester, or Chicago.

Above: *Magnetic resonance imaging (MRI) at Sioux Valley Hospital.*

Facing page: *The ever-sprawling McKennan Hospital campus.*

ITS SOURCES OF WEALTH.

The advancement of Sioux Falls has never been of that spasmodic variety which has characterized so many western communities. Since 1876 the development has been steady and continuous, each year seeing the community more firmly established than the preceding. The possession of such a complete assortment of those elements which are the foundations f prosperity, has given a feeling of certainty to all concerned, and has stimulated enterprises for developing and taking advantage of them.

—*E.W. CALDWELL*
Sioux Falls Illustrated, *1888*

While most of us serenely minded our own business, the city of Sioux Falls quietly established itself as a major regional medical center. Procedures, facilities, and services that once required patients to journey to Minneapolis, Rochester, or Denver now exist in Sioux Falls. To a great extent, the city is a destination, not a departure point, for those seeking medical treatment. Hospitals, clinics, and other health-related facilities see well in excess of 100,000 inpatients and outpatients every year and are in an almost ceaseless state of construction, expansion, and development. Every third or fourth person you meet, it sometimes seems, is involved at least peripherally in providing health-care or wellness services.

As with so much in this community, Sioux Falls' emergence as a health-care center occurred fairly quietly—so much so that a person may be excused for thinking it happened overnight—and not at all by accident.

Currently there are two major general hospitals in Sioux Falls, both privately owned. Sioux Valley Hospital can trace its roots back to the Sioux Falls Hospital, which existed in one form or another—and usually in large rented houses—from

1894 until 1901, at which time it settled into permanent quarters at Nineteenth Street and Minnesota Avenue. In 1930, the Sioux Falls Hospital merged with Bethany Hospital—one of many smaller private hospitals that existed here when the 20th century was young—to form Sioux Valley Hospital, with new facilities at Eighteenth Street and Grange Avenue, the heart of the present hospital's ever-growing "campus."

Meanwhile, at the other end of town—or so it must have seemed at the time, although in reality the distance was and is only a couple of miles—McKennan Hospital began seeing patients in 1911, thanks, as we have seen, to a $25,000 bequest left by Helen Gale McKennan. McKennan Hospital was and is operated by the Catholic Church, managed by the Presentation Sisters of Aberdeen, South Dakota.

For many years, the people of Sioux Falls tended to regard these two entities, Sioux Valley and McKennan, as competitors, albeit in a somewhat lopsided manner, since McKennan was considered "the Catholic hospital" and Sioux Valley the "every-other-belief hospital." Actually, a fair number of people around here *still* think that way—and, it must be said, the two institutions themselves have not always gone out of their way to discourage that kind of thinking. Which is why some residents, even lifelong residents, are surprised to learn that the city's current status as a regional medical center resulted from a long history of cooperation between the two competitors.

Nearly thirty years ago, after

Sioux Falls—the most noticeable effect is that the two hospitals tend to alternate their major building projects. Of course, every big hospital in every city is *always* under construction to a greater or lesser extent—where do you suppose anyone ever got the idea that hospitals are "quiet

have the new machine that goes beep-beep-beep, Sioux Valley installs an open-heart surgery unit while McKennan introduces laser surgery for eye patients, and so on. Today, Sioux Valley Hospital, with 476 patient beds, is known for cardiac care, neonatal care (including infant intensive-care), and same-day surgery, among other specialties; McKennan Hospital, with 409 beds, emphasizes cancer treatment and care, mental health, and family-centered childbirth.

Today, EROS manages the world's largest collection of earth images acquired from space or from aircraft—10.2 million frames of photographic data and more than 152,000 digital tapes, but who's counting?

---

several expansion projects at each hospital, Sioux Valley and McKennan hired an independent consultant to study the region, the city, and the hospitals in order to help the hospitals develop a plan for future growth and modernization. Rather than squander resources and energy trying constantly to one-up the other, each hospitals would, to an extent, develop its own areas of specialization; although still technically in competition, they would work in concert to build a state-of-the-art medical facility for the region.

To the outsider—which is to say, to the average citizen of

zones?"—but for the past twenty or twenty-five years, McKennan Hospital and Sioux Valley Hospital have undertaken their big construction projects on a staggered schedule, with one beginning its building phase only when the other has completed its own.

More important, in terms of the care being delivered, the hospitals also have worked in concert to bring to Sioux Falls cutting-edge medical technology. (Get it? Cutting-edge—a little surgical humor there.) Again, a kind of rotation is involved, so that rather than each hospital trying to outdo the other by being the first to

It all sounds very civilized— and, of course, it's hard to argue with the very obvious and very beneficial success that the hospitals' cooperation has had—but it would be overstating the case to pretend that the two entities are not, at heart, competitors, whose areas of service frequently overlap. Both hospitals fairly tripped over each other a few years ago, when helicopters were all the rage, to get theirs. (At least they use them—as I can readily attest, since our house is roughly midway between the two hospitals!) Shortly afterward, they fomented a tempest in a teacup when McKennan began billing itself as the proud owner of the region's only "trauma center," strongly implying that a plain old garden-variety emergency room—like Sioux Valley's, for instance—was by comparison second-rate. I mention these instances not only because they're fun, but also to illustrate that, while cooperation may have been the most important element in taking Sioux Falls to its current position as a regional medical center, it wasn't the sole element. Healthy competition played its part, too, and still does. (Healthy competition: more medical humor.)

Of course, there's more to it than the two hospitals. A glance at the phone book indicates the existence of roughly fifty medical clinics, some in loose association with the hospitals, some not—and that *doesn't* include dentistry, chiropractic, optometry, physical therapy, mental-health, or wellness centers. Especially worthy of note are McGreevy Clinic and Central Plains Clinic, each within a stone's throw of McKennan Hospital; Dakota Midwest Cancer Institute on the McKennan campus; North Central Heart Institute and Sioux Falls Neurosurgery, on the Sioux Valley campus; and Van Demark Bone & Joint Clinic.

There are about 400 medical doctors in Sioux Falls, plus a varying number of medical school residents, which proba-

bly explains why the city keeps having to add golf courses. In addition to McKennan Hospital and Sioux Valley Hospital, Sioux Falls also is home to the Royal C. Johnson Veterans Hospital, with 269 patient beds; the Crippled Children's Hospital and School, with 96 beds, and Charter Hospital, a mental-health facility, with 60 beds.

The University of South Dakota School of Medicine, though "officially" located on the USD campus in Vermillion, South Dakota, some sixty miles south of here, is also a major player in the regional medical center that Sioux Falls has become. The School of Medicine has been instrumental not only in producing new physicians, many of whom continue to practice in and around the city, but also in bringing to Sioux Falls the sorts of research programs that go hand in hand with medical centers. Currently the School of Medicine is completing a $6-million health center in Sioux Falls, on the Sioux Valley Hospital Campus, which will provide examination rooms for ambulatory-care patients, classrooms, and offices for USD medical school faculty in Sioux Falls.

It's interesting to note, in all this talk of Sioux Falls' posi-

tion as a regional medical center, that the state of South Dakota entered the medical sweepstakes in a big way only within the past twenty years. Prior to 1974, the USD School of Medicine offered only a two-year medical program, which forced students to transfer to medical schools elsewhere to finish their education. Eventually it dawned on someone that people have a tendency to settle wherever they happen to be when they get out of school, or, in the case of physicians, when they finish residency, and that if you wanted to keep doctors in South Dakota, perhaps a good first step would be to not encourage them to leave in the first place! The legislature approved the establishment of USD's four-year medical program only in 1974!

Viewed in that light, the city's emergence as a force in regional health-care is even more remarkable.

Shortly after my wife and I moved back to Sioux Falls in 1985, I was on the phone with my literary agent and mentioned that I had an upcoming book-signing scheduled at "one of the local bookstores." He laughed, and said he was surprised to learn that Sioux Falls had more than one bookstore. I let his remark pass without comment, since I long ago

Above: *Although the first airport in Sioux Falls was built in 1929, it took World War II and the establishment of a Radio Technical Training School at the Sioux Falls Air Base to put the city on the aeronautic map. Today, Northwest, TWA, United, American, and several regional airlines connect Joe Foss Field to the world's airways.*

Left: *Manufacturing is the city's third-largest employment sector, accounting for more than 8,300 jobs.*

MIKE ROEMER PHOTOS

96

learned how deeply some inhabitants of larger cities—New York, in this case—cherish their geographical ignorance. There are still plenty of people whose minds, upon receiving the words "Sioux Falls," conjure up that "Little House on the Prairie" image. And not all of those people have the excuse of being New Yorkers, either—some of them are Chicagoans, Minneapolitans, Omahans, and other near-neighbors who should know better!

I mention this not only to have some fun at my agent's expense (former agent, but that has nothing to do with the Sioux Falls incident), but also by way of bracing you for another revelation about Sioux Falls: This is not only a medical center, but also a technology center.

It began twenty years ago, with the opening of the Earth Resources Observation Systems (EROS) Data Center sixteen miles northeast of Sioux Falls. (Actually, it began in 1971, when EROS operated out of temporary offices in Sioux Falls proper, but that's not nearly as momentous-sounding.) EROS falls under the purview of the U.S. Geological Survey, which in turn falls under the Department of the Interior, and somehow the Na-

tional Mapping Division works itself in there. And none of it explains what EROS is or does.

A few years ago, my wife overheard a couple of women talking about EROS. One of them asked what it stood for, and the other replied without hesitation: "Earth's Resources in Outer Space." Which isn't too far off the beam. EROS began in the early seventies to "receive, process, and distribute data" from NASA's Landsat satellites. Today, EROS manages the world's largest collection of earth images acquired from space or from aircraft—10.2 million frames of photographic data and more than 152,000 digital tapes, but who's counting? If you've ever seen one of those as-seen-from-space pictures of a city or region where the water is black and the vegetation is pink, you've probably been looking at an EROS-processed image. Remember those similarly surreal images showing the effects of the Kuwait oil fires on the Middle East? EROS. The images were relayed from a remote-sensing satellite joyriding along some 425 miles above the planet to the EROS Data Center computers right here on the lone prairie, and thence to the world.

On the one hand, it's no accident that the EROS Data Center came to be located

here: it's no secret that the city and the state campaigned long and hard to attract the facility. On the other hand, though, it *is* sort of an accident—an accident of geography, of the sort that has played such an important part in the history of Sioux Falls. The Geological Survey needed a site that was fairly open yet not completely remote, centrally located, and free of obstructions that would block signals from orbiting satellites. As was the case in 1856, Sioux Falls was in the right place at the right time.

Currently, EROS employs nearly 400 scientists, engineers, and technicians at its 318-acre facility outside of the city. It's involved in research into agricultural development, forest change, natural disasters, water resources, and urban growth; and it supplied satellite images to the military during Operation Desert Storm. In addition, the United Nations Environmental Programme/Global Resource Information Database (UNEP/GRID) has a North America Node office at the EROS Data Center, one of several around the world that provide environmental data for U.N. member nations.

But don't just take my word for it: The EROS Data is open

Both pages: The Earth Resources Observation Systems (EROS) Data Center, northeast of Sioux Falls, founded to "receive, process, and distribute data" from NASA's Landsat satellites, and home of the world's largest collection of earth images acquired from space or aircraft.

during the week, and offers a public informational program.

Another aspect of all these high-tech high-jinks is reflected in the emergence of the Queen City as a regional financial center. In a sense, it has always been so. After all, the city was literally founded in real-estate, and even in the 19th century, banking, insurance, and other financial undertakings figured prominently into the local economy, if for no other reason than Sioux Falls' being the state's largest population center and the seat of Minnehaha County.

But all of it shifted into top gear in early 1981, when Citibank came to town. Citibank is the credit-card division of Citicorp, the New York financial giant. If your mail brings you an invitation to acquire a Citibank Visa card, you will see that the envelope is pre-addressed to "Citibank (South Dakota) N.A."—and also to a mailing center in Maryland or some-

place, but then I've never pretended to understand why big businesses do the things they do. The point is, Citibank runs its entire credit-card operation from its facility in an industrial park on the north side of Sioux Falls.

It would be nice to pretend that Citicorp decided to move Citibank here because we're a bunch of swell people and they thought they'd like to get to know us better. Undoubtedly that was *part* of the reason, but we must cynically acknowledge that, in the early 1980s, the South Dakota legislature relaxed many regulations pertaining to financial institutions—and, not the least, raised the limit on interest rates charged by credit-card companies—with the express purpose of attracting such businesses to the state. Today, Citibank employs some 2,800 workers, making it the second-largest employer in town (Sioux Valley Hospital employs about 100 more). It relies on state-of-the-art computer, telephonic, and satellite technology in order to conduct its business. And high-tech breeds high-tech. Because of the volume of Citibank mail streaming through here, the U.S. Postal Service in Sioux Falls utilizes more sophisticated mail-handling equipment and technologies than in most other cities of this size, which in turn is expected to eventually attract other mail-intensive businesses to town.

While much is made of Sioux Falls' success in attracting "weather-proof" financial businesses—keeping in mind that no more than fifteen or twenty years ago, the local economy lived and died on the vicissitudes of agriculture—not even high-finance is immune to the slings and arrows of outrageous fortune. For instance, in 1984 Sioux Falls scored another coup when the large First National Bank of Houston located its national credit-card operation here. By all accounts, First City (as the credit-card division was known) held its own, but the rigors of the Texas economy in the late 1980s—when oil prices and real-estate prices managed to go directions they weren't supposed to—took their toll on the parent corporation. First City's headquarters, a stunning office building located on the southern edge of the city, just off Interstate 29, is being converted into offices for the Good Samaritan Society (which also is based here, by the way).

On the plus side, Sears located a regional credit-card facility here several years ago, and if persistent unfounded rumors that Sears plans to move its national credit-card operation here, or its Discover card operation—or both—obstinately refuse to come true, well, at least it's not beyond the realm of possibility anymore!

99

Going from Today

Beginning in 1890, the South Dakota Rapid Transit Company operated an "electric motor line" between Sioux Falls and East Sioux Falls. Within the city itself, horse-drawn and electric cars were run by the Sioux Falls Street Railway Company from 1887 until 1889, and by the Sioux Falls Traction System from 1907 until 1930, when the streetcars gave way to "motor buses."

Sioux Falls, South Dakota.

In the preceding pages, I have tried to convey a sense of this community in these early days of its second century. I have tried to be honest; I have tried to be fair; I have tried to be complete. But of course a city of the size of Sioux Falls, a city growing as rapidly as Sioux Falls, a city with so much history behind it and so much more history ahead of it virtually defies description. In the end, I think, a city cannot be described; it can only be experienced. And experiences are unique to the individual.

Therefore, what you have in these pages is "my" Sioux Falls, captured as if in a photograph, framed in the viewfinder that is my eye and mind, frozen at this instant in time. Of necessity, then, the city has changed, however slightly, in just the few moments that we have been discussing it.

Observant soul that you are, you will undoubtedly have noticed that we leapfrogged over, oh, roughly eighty years of history, from Sioux Falls' infancy, in the late 19th and early 20th centuries, to its adolescence in the late 20th century. We did

this for two reasons: First, this ain't no history book; and, second, there are plenty of very good histories of Sioux Falls and the region, and yours truly has never seen much sport in reinventing the wheel. So, naturally, there are signal events in Sioux Falls' childhood, events that to a greater or lesser extent formed the city that exists today—and events that we quite purposely skipped.

For instance, we didn't talk about Sioux Falls' reputation as a "divorce mill" in the late 1800s and early 1900s. State law set legal residency at six months, as opposed to a year in most states, and since Sioux Falls was the largest city in the state, it was only natural for people—some of them quite affluent—to set up here for the requisite period. This was quite a booming little industry for the town, naturally enough, since the "temporary residents" needed places to live, food to eat, clothes to wear, and so on. But the boom didn't last terribly long. By 1908, the period for legal residency had been increased to a full year, and the divorce mill closed.

We barely mentioned the coming of the railroad in 1878; we didn't talk about the first horse-drawn streetcars that began operation in 1887; or how telephone service began as early as 1882; or how homes could be supplied with water, gas, and electricity by 1890.

We didn't talk about the meat-packing industry, which began in the 1880s, sort of sputtered along for a couple of decades, and then became important—indeed, cardinal—to the local economy with the opening of the John Morrell Packing Company in 1909. The Morrell plant, for many years the city's biggest employer and still a key economic player, is in operation yet today.

We didn't talk about the Great Depression, the Dust Bowl Days, the hoards of grasshoppers that virtually denuded this agricultural state in the Dirty Thirties. The psychological impact on the residents must have been incalculable; certainly the economic impact was devastating. But the Depression brought about recovery efforts such as PWA and WPA, each of which left a physical mark on the city—roads, bridges, buildings, many of which are still in use today.

We didn't talk about World War II, which, in a sense, is when Sioux Falls started to be a "real" city. The war brought about the establishment of a Radio Technical Training School for the Army Air Corps at the Sioux Falls airport; during the peak of the war effort,

more than 20,000 military and civilian personnel were associated with the Air Base—which had the effect not only of increasing Sioux Falls' population by half again but also of exposing the local folks to large numbers of "outsiders," men and women from all over the United States, people who spoke with different regional accents and came from different backgrounds and had different ideas and goals than the still-quite-homogeneous people of Sioux Falls. Of course, there was a significant economic impact as well—you don't bring 20,000 people to a town without the town experiencing a serious boom—but I can't help but think that the psychological impact, the cultural impact, must have had equally long-lasting effects. Certainly it would have broadened residents' minds. Perhaps it broadened their horizons as well—perhaps that experience set the stage for modern Sioux Falls' entry into the ranks of important American cities.

And what of modern Sioux Falls—since, after all, that's our concern here. It is, as I indicated at the outset, a city in flux, an adolescent city in the sense that it's too big to be a "town" but lacks the experience of an older, larger city. It is a city torn between those

who would keep it anchored in the recent past and those who would shove it headlong into the future—that is, those who think the city is already "too darn big" and those who think the city isn't getting big enough and sophisticated enough fast enough.

Politically, Sioux Falls is fairly conservative—as is the entire region. There has never been a powerful political "machine" here, but as in most American cities there has existed and to an extent still exists a certain amount of cronyism. Less so year by year, I think, as the city grows not just in terms of population but in terms of the diversity of the population, and the cronies find their influence diluted.

And yet, somewhat paradoxically, there is a deep-seated populist attitude here. You may remember from your history classes that South Dakota gave us the initiative and the referendum, and both devices are used extensively here to this day. It's a fairly safe bet that, anytime a halfway controversial decision emerges from the City Commission, someone will circulate a petition to refer the matter to a vote of the people. The civic-minded citizen must simply resign him- or herself to spending an awful lot of time in the voting booth.

Above: *The meat-packing industry became a cornerstone of the local economy when the John Morrell Packing Company opened here in 1909. The Sioux Falls plant is the flagship of the Morrell operation, and the city's second-biggest employer. (Beyond the plant is downtown, with the US West Building most prominent.)*

Facing page: *As Sioux Falls has grown as a regional financial center, so too have sprung up the imposing edifices of banks, brokerages, insurance companies, and related businesses.*

At the moment, Sioux Falls is governed by a full-time mayor and four full-time commissioners, elected at-large (the mayor is considered a commissioner). The current system went into place only a handful of years ago (for half a century it was a three-member commission), and may be scrapped by the time you read this. A citizen's group is circulating yet another petition, this one calling for a vote to change the form of government to one of a picturesque town, a fact that I hope has come across in our tour of some of the neighborhoods. A very green city—well, for five or six months of the year, anyway. The rest of the time it's usually a very *white* city. Most of the people take good care of their property—lawns are mowed, bushes are trimmed, houses are painted. The crime rate is below the national average. So is unemployment: 2.8 percent, compared to a national aver- western city that boasts a recent unemployment rate of 2.6 percent." The authors pointed out, rightly, that "this former cow town" has "one of the most diverse and robust economies" in the country.

The survey took readers' most important concerns—44 issues including clean water (the most important issue), low crime rate (a close second) health facilities, education, cultural and recreational opportunities, and so on. Then *Money's* editors compared the list with data on each of the 300 largest cities, following up with a visit to the top five. When everything was added up and averaged out, Sioux Falls scored 70 percent on health; 47 percent on crime, 100 percent on economy; 75 percent on housing; 28 percent on education; 98 percent on transit; 22 percent on weather; 2 percent on leisure; and 10 percent on arts. It may sound petty to complain—after all, we *did* come in number one—but you have to wonder, given what we've discussed about this city's health-care industry and recreational options, how on earth the magazine came up with only 70 percent for health and 2 percent for leisure!

Such rankings are always a little surreal, of course. Sioux

Because it's all there, the resources natural, human, and economic, swirling about in anticipation of the right concentrations and the right conditions and exactly the right moment for the event—Spontaneous combustion.

---

full-time mayor and eight part-time commissioners, elected by ward. It would take a book much thicker than this one to discuss all of the various forms of municipal government that have existed in Sioux Falls since those first land-company agents arrived, so you will find here no prediction as to what form of government the city may have by the end of the 20th century.

Sioux Falls is a pretty town, age of 6.4 percent. Other cities in the region have been plagued by influxes of street gangs, but so far Sioux Falls has been spared that.

In its September 1992 issue, *Money* magazine presented its sixth annual "Best Places to Live in America" survey. To the surprise, no doubt, of many across the country, Sioux Falls placed first. The *Money* article called it a "friendly, little-known mid-

Falls wasn't a noticeably better place to live in 1992 than it had been in 1991, and it wasn't noticeably worse in 1993 than it had been in 1992, so how did it come to be "the Best Place to Live in America" that year and (so far) that year only? And how did it come to drop to ninth place the following year? Did those other eight cities really get *that much better* in so short a time? Well, anyhow, it was fun while it lasted; the city and the city's social-service agencies seem able to cope with the increased numbers of people who flocked here looking for gold-paved streets; and it was nice to have a nationally prominent business publication confirm what many of us had long suspected.

Sioux Falls is an exciting city. I realize that many of my fellow residents, and many former residents, will find that statement amusing, but I respectfully suggest that those people have Portland cement between their ears and as a consequence have no imagination. For of course Sioux Falls isn't an exciting city in the sense that Las Vegas is an exciting city. It's not that obvious. It's not that immediate. The excitement is in the future. It goes back to that kinetic energy we talked about in the beginning.

Think of how the Falls must have looked to those early settlers. The rush and roll and roar of water. The untapped power. The limitless potential. The unimagined—perhaps even unimaginable—possibilities. All of that kinetic energy, just waiting for someone to figure out how to plug into and put to use.

Now fast-forward nearly a century and a half. The City of Sioux Falls, I think, should be looked at the same way those early pioneers looked at the city's namesake. In terms of potential. In terms of possibilities. In terms of energy just waiting to be tapped. Because it's all there, the resources natural, human, and economic, swirling about in anticipation of the right concentrations and the right conditions and exactly the right moment for the event—Spontaneous combustion.

Or not.

If we look to the Falls again, we have to remember that all of that potential, all of that energy, was never really successfully exploited. People tried; people failed.

And so it could go with the Queen City, too. Our having the resources by no means guarantees that we will be able to combine them in just the proper fashion to achieve

whatever we may hope to achieve—in a year, a decade, a half-century. It's a complex formula, and unfortunately no one's ever written it down. The people of every community have to invent it as they go along, and you never know whether it's going to work. Like the kinetic energy of the Falls, the kinetic energy of Sioux Falls may never be successfully realized.

And then again—it may! It could all be coming together, below the surface, right at this very moment. Or next year. Or ten years from now…

Now, tell me this isn't an exciting city!

A Reasonable Deduction.
If, then, it is demonstrated that there is a field here for enterprise, energy, industry and exercise of good judgment in all directions in which such qualities can be brought into play, does it not follow as a matter of course that good men desiring to improve their conditions and surrounding can secure better opportunities in Sioux Falls than at any other point toward which attention has been so persistently directed?…It is to such a locality as this that a visit is invited. Come and inspect it for yourself.
—E.W. Caldwell
Sioux Falls Illustrated, *1888*

Above: *The Minnehaha Country Club, seen here one misty morning, and the adjacent Westward Ho Country Club and Sherman Park Complex together form a bucolic, peaceful oasis in the midst of the fast-growing city.*

Facing page: *having made its way over the cataracts, the Big Sioux River continues through a gorge just below the Falls.* JEFF GNASS

Where Credit Is Due

Sioux Falls is about 140 years old. I've lived here, off and on, for about eighteen of the past twenty-eight years. Which means that not everything herein comes first-hand from me!

The number of books and other publications about the history of Sioux Falls and environs is surprisingly large. Even larger is the number of books about South Dakota as a whole. I read, or read in, scores of such books while preparing background for *Sioux Falls: The City and the People*. The following works were of particular help—or, if not very helpful, were at least interesting—and I unhesitatingly recommend them:

Bragstad, R.E. *Sioux Falls in Retrospect*. Privately published, 1967.

Caldwell, E.W. *Sioux Falls Illustrated: A Comprehensive Sketch of the City's Wonderful Growth and its Resources*. Omaha: D. C. Dunbar & Co., 1888.

Fanebust, Wayne. *Where the Sioux River Bends: A Newspaper Chronicle*. Freeman, SD: Pine Hill Press, 1984.

Karolevitz , Robert F. *Challenge: The South Dakota Story*. Sioux Falls: Brevet Press, 1975.

Milton, John R. *South Dakota: A History*. New York: W.W. Norton, 1977.

Parker, Donald Dean. *Pioneering in the Upper Sioux Valley: Medary, Sioux Falls, Dell Rapids, Flandreau, Brookings, Watertown*. Privately published, 1967.

Planning and Building Services Department of the City of Sioux Falls. *Historic Avenues in Sioux Falls, South Dakota*. Sioux Falls: City of Sioux Falls, 1983.

Finally, there are several individuals who assisted in this endeavor, so I would like to acknowledge those contributions:

Mr. Ron Beck, Earth Resources Observation Satellite Data Center, who provided much valuable information about EROS.

Mr. Doug Murdock, Sioux Falls Public Library, who was there at the beginning—before the beginning!—and several points following.

Mr. Gary Weckwerth, General Manager, Sioux Falls Canaries, who supplied current information as well as some of the history of the team.

Mr. Scott Strain, who supplied research materials and moral support.

And my dad, who probably did not realize before now that I actually was listening to all those stories and anecdotes…

Index

Italics indicate illustration

Agriculture 7, 18
All Saints neighborhood 55–59
All Saints School 55–58, 90
Allen, Capt. Joseph 19
Amidon, J.B. 25
Arikara Indians 17
Astor, John Jacob 61
Augustana College 51, 75, *89*, 90, 91

Baker, William L. 63
Ballard, Levi W. 58
Baptist Church 89
Barn Theater 75
Bennett Quarry 42
Big Sioux River: and early people 17, 19, 24; described 41; formation 12; navigation 20; parks 79; pictured *4, 56, 71, 106*
Big Sioux River Recreation Trail 86, 87
Bike Trail 86
Brockhouse, Henry 77
Brookings, W.W. 48, 54
Business Men's League of Sioux Falls 47

Caldwell, E.W. 16, 72, 92, 105
Calvary Episcopal Cathedral *60*
Canaries pro baseball team *78*, 85
Cascade Milling Company 34
Cataract Hotel 49
Cathedral Historic District 53–54
Catholic Church *48*, 54, 93–94
Center for Western Studies 77
Central Fire Station 38
Central Plains Clinic 95
Charter Hospital 95
Chicago St. Paul Minneapolis and Omaha Railway Co. 34
Churches *15, 33, 48, 49, 60*
Citibank 51, 98–99
City Auditorium 47, *82*

City Hall *45*, 47
Civic Fine Arts Center 75
Climate 10, 80, 87
Coats Quarry 42
Community Concert Association 74
Corn Palace, World's Only 83
Coughran, Edward 62
Coughran, Edward, house *37*
Covell Lake *36*, 82
Crippled Children's Hospital and School 95

Dakota (Santee Sioux) 17
Dakota Collegiate Institute 89
Dakota Land Company 21–24, 29
Dakota Midwest Cancer Institute 95
Dakota Relays 85
Dakota String Quartet 74
Dakota Woodwind Quintet 74
"David" sculpture 51, *61*
Daytrips 83
Delbridge family 78
Delbridge Museum of Natural History 70, 77–78
Depression years 25, 101
Divorce mill 100
Dow, W.L. 44, 58, 90
Downtown (described) 42–53
Dunbar Hospital 58–59
Dust Bowl 101

Earth Resources Observation Systems (EROS) 97–98, *98*
Eide/Dalrymple Gallery 77
El Riad Circus 85
Empire Mall 46, 86
Employment: breakdown 7; Citibank 99; EROS 97; John Morrell Co. 42, 101, *102*; manufacturing 96
Enchanted World Doll Museum 83

Episcopal Church 58
EROS. *See* Earth Resources Observation Systems
Ethnic groups 34, 54

Falls Park 39, 42, 86
Farwell, James 24
Fawick Flyer 50, 51
Fawick Park *3, 61*
Fawick, Thomas 50, 51, 61
Federal Building 50
Fenn Brothers Ice Cream and Confectionery Company 63
Fenn, Henry C. 63
Ferris, Jacob 19
First National Bank 49
Fiske, J.L. 24
Flandreau, South Dakota 83
Fort Brookings 28
Fort Dakota 28, 36, 50, 90
Fort Sod 57
Freeze dates 87
Fremont, Gen. John C. 19
Friends of Traditional Music 74

Gale, Artemus 59
Garretson, South Dakota 83
Geography 7, 9
Geology 9–12, *13*
German immigrants 34, 54
Golf courses 84, 107
Good Samaritan Society 99
Government 34, 104
Great Bear Ski Valley 82
Great Northern Railway 35
Great Plains Balloon Race 66
Great Plains Zoo 70, 78–79, 87
Greenway 86, 87
Grigsby, Melvin 59–60
Grigsby, Sioux 62

Hare, William H., Bishop 58, 61, 90
Harrington, Delores 62

Hawthorne Elementary School 55
Health care 92–95
Heynsohn brothers 55
History 17–32
Hollister Brothers Loan Company
    62
Hollister, F.H. 62
Hospitals 58, 92–95
Howard, C.K. 90
Howard Wood Dakota Relays 85
Howe, Oscar 83
Huron University 91

Indians. See Native Americans

John Morrell Packing Company
    42, 101, 102

Kilian Community College 91

Lakota Indians 17–19, 18, 25
Lein, Burre 62
Lein/Hollister House 62
Leisure activities 72–86
Lewis & Clark Recreation Area
    74, 83
Lewis and Clark Expedition 19
Lutheran Church 54, 89
Lutheran Normal Training School
    90

McBride, James 24
McClellan, John 21, 48, 54
McGarraugh Quarry 42
McGreevy Clinic 95
McKennan, Helen Gale 59, 63, 93
McKennan Hospital 63, 93, 93–95
McKennan Park 10, 27, 60–62, 61
McKennan Park neighborhood 55,
    59–63
Mandan Indians 17
Master Singers 74
Meat-packing industry 101

Medical facilities 92–95
Memorial to the Pioneers 18
Midland National Life 57
Millard, Ezra 19, 21, 49
Milwaukee Railway Company 35,
    42
Minerva's Restaurant 86
Minnehaha Country Club 84, 107
Minnehaha County 7, 24, 54, 98
Minnehaha County Courthouse
    33, 44, 75
Minnehaha Springs 54, 55
Minnesota Avenue 53
Mitchell, South Dakota 83
Monarch Quarries 42
Money magazine 6, 7, 15, 104–
    105
Morrell. See John Morrell Packing
    Company
"Moses" sculpture 51

Nakota (Yankton Sioux) 17
National Butter Makers Associa-
    tion 47
National College 91
Native Americans 17–19, 24, 25,
    49, 83
Neighborhoods 36–63
Nettleton Junior College 91
Newton Hills State Park 83
Nicollet, Joseph 12, 19, 23
Ninth Street 36, 38, 54
Norman B. Mears Library 77
North American Baptist Seminary
    91
North Central Heart Institute 95
North End 52–55, 82
Northern Plains Gallery 75
Northern Plains Tribal Arts Show
    and Market 85
Northern States Power 42
Norwegian Evangelical Lutheran
    Synod 90

Norwegian immigrants 34
Norwest Bank 49, 65

Ojibwa 17
Old Courthouse and Warehouse
    Historic District 43
Old Courthouse Museum 33, 46,
    75
Olde Town Theatre 75
Oleson, Halvor 24
Orpheum Theatre 44, 81
Oscar Howe Art Center 83

Palisades State Park 83
Parade of Lights 84
Parks: Covell Lake 82; drives to
    83; Falls 39, 42, 86; Fawick 3,
    51, 61; McKennan 10, 27, 55,
    60, 61; Sherman 78, 79–82,
    107; Spellerberg 6; Terrace
    82; Tuthill 82; Van Eps 81
Pettigrew Home and Museum 41,
    54, 75
Pettigrew, R.F. 41, 54, 75, 89
Phillips Avenue 36, 39, 42, 46, 49,
    50
Phillips House 38
Phillips, J.L. 29, 35
Pillars of the Nation 62
Politics 30, 101
Population 7–8, 63
Precipitation, annual average 87
Preemption Act of 1841 20–21, 31
Prehistoric people 16–17
Presentation Sisters of Aberdeen
    93
Prohibition 43

Quarrying industry 13, 20, 42
Queen Bee Mill 8, 34, 41, 43

Radio Technical Training School
    96, 101

No matter how "citified" Sioux Falls grows, a short drive in any direction reminds that this is indeed the Heartland.

Railroads 16, 21, 34, 100
Religions 15, 54, 58, 61, 89, *93*
Restaurants 86
Rock Island Railway 35
Royal C. Johnson Veterans
    Hospital 95
Royal River Casino 83

St. Joseph Cathedral *33*, *48*, *49*, 54
St. Michael's Pro-Cathedral 49
St. Patrick's Day parade 50, 84
Santee Sioux 25
Scandinavian immigrants 54
Schaetzel, Jacob, Jr. 34
Schools *41*, 75, 88–91
"Sea Dreams" sculpture *57*
Seasons 87
Security Bank Building 47, *65*

Seney, A.G. 42
Seney Island 42
Seney Quarry 42
Sherman, E.A. 60, 90
Sherman Park Complex *78*, 79,
    79–82, 107
Shoto-teien Japanese Tea Gardens
    82
Shriver-Johnson Building 50
Sidewalk Arts Festival 85
Singing Boys of Sioux Falls 74
Sioux Empire Entertainment
    League 75, 80
Sioux Empire Fair *64*, 74, 85
Sioux Empire Farm Show 85
Sioux Falls Air Base 96
Sioux Falls Bottling Works 55
Sioux Falls Brewery 43

Sioux Falls Canaries *78*, 85
Sioux Falls College 75, 77, 89, 91
Sioux Falls Community Playhouse
    44, 75, *81*
Sioux Falls Granite: buildings of
    41, 42, 44, 51; described 12,
    39; Palisades State Park
    83; quarrying *13*, *20*, 42
Sioux Falls Granite Company *40*,
    44
Sioux Falls Illustrated (1888) 16,
    72, 92, 105
Sioux Falls Jasper. *See* Sioux Falls
    Granite
Sioux Falls Master Singers 74
Sioux Falls Municipal Band 62
Sioux Falls Neurosurgery 95
Sioux Falls of the Big Sioux River:

and town companies 21; de-
scribed 12–15, 39–42; energy
potential 34; pictured *5, 8, 11,
23, 30, 68*
Sioux Falls Skyforce *76*, 85
Sioux Falls Stockyards 7, 42
Sioux Falls Street Railway Com-
pany 100
Sioux Falls Traction System 100
Sioux Granite. *See* Sioux Falls
Granite
Sioux peoples 17–19
Sioux Valley Hospital *92*, 92–95
Siouxland Heritage Museums 75
Skyforce 76, 85
Smith, Charles A. 24
Soukup & Thomas Balloon and
Airship Museum 83
South Dakota Rapid Transit
Company 100
South Dakota School for the Deaf
90
South Dakota Symphony 74
Southeast Technical Institute 91
Spellerberg Park 6
Split Rock Creek 83
Sports, professional *78*, 85

Spring Avenue 55
Staples, George M. 19
Stenotype Institute of South
Dakota 91
Stewart School of Hairstyling 91
Streetcars 100
Sun days per year 87
Swedish immigrants 34

Tate, Samuel L. 90
Tea (town) 75
Temperature, average annual 87
Terrace Park 82
Teton Sioux 17
Thomas, Steve 57
Town companies 19–25, 29, 31
Tuthill Park 82

U.S.S. South Dakota Memorial *78*
U.S.S. South Dakota battleship 79
University of South Dakota School
of Medicine 95
US West 47, *102*

Van Demark Bone & Joint Clinic
95
Van Eps Park 81

W.H. Lyon Fairgrounds *64*
Washington Pavilion of Arts and
Sciences 51
Washington Senior High School
51
Weatherwax, F.H., Clothing Store
63
Weatherwax, Frank H. 63
West Sioux Hardware 77
Western Bank *44*, 49
Western Mall 46
Western Town Company 19–21,
29, 54
Westward Ho Country Club 84,
107
Whittier Middle School *41*
Wind speed, average annual 87
Works Progress Administration
(WPA) *45*, 47, 101
Worthing, South Dakota 75

Yankton Lakota 24, 25
YMCA 84

Zandbroz Variety 50

About The Author

William J. Reynolds is best known for his mystery novels and short stories, the latest of which are Drive-by *and "The Lost Boys" (in the anthology* The Mysterious West, *edited by Tony Hillerman and Martin H. Greenberg). Reynolds has a strong attachment to his hometown. It's where he learned to drive, where he had his first date, and where he met his wife, Peg. They are still in Sioux Falls living happily ever after with their two children, Meredith and Will.*